The QUEENS OF ANCIENT EGYPT

WHITE STAR PUBLISHERS

H.E. MRS. SUZANNE MUBARAK

Some of ancient Egypt's most famous queens are known to us for their beauty, others for their power. The portrait bust of Nefertiti is thought by many to represent the most beautiful woman the world has ever known, and Hatshepsut ruled as a monarch in her own right, performing the regal duties of a male pharaoh. We think of Cleopatra as a legendary beauty, but her military exploits and political maneuvering are equally a part of her tale. These well-known royal women of ancient Egypt, and others not as familiar to us, are brought to life in the pages of this splendid book in images that depict their grace and majesty, their strength and dignity, with accompanying text that explores their stories.

Most of Egypt's ancient queens played a central role along with the pharaoh to whom they were connected by marriage or by birth. They seem to have enjoyed a higher status than their contemporaries in other lands, and like many modern women, had to balance the duties of motherhood with the more public responsibilities of work. Often, these royal women exercised power as regents for their sons who were too young to rule. I like to think that these ancient queens so dedicated to public service are an inspiration for the women in our society today who have achieved influential positions as judges, corporate leaders, politicians, and government ministers.

I invite you to linger over the glorious photographs of sculpture, tomb paintings, exquisite jewelry, and other treasures from Egypt's cultural heritage that specifically celebrate the female side of the throne. It is easy to imagine that William Shakespeare might have been describing all these ancient queens, not just Cleopatra, when he wrote "Age cannot wither her, nor custom stale her infinite variety."

Suzanne Mubarak

foreword
H.E. MRS. SUZANNE MUBARAK

introduction
DOROTHEA ARNOLD

texts
ROSANNA PIRELLI

editorial director
VALERIA MANFERTO DE FABIANIS

editorial coordination
LAURA ACCOMAZZO
GIORGIO FERRERO

graphic design
MARINELLA DEBERNARDI

4-5 BUST OF QUEEN NEFERTITI (ÄGYPTISCHES MUSEUM, BERLIN).

7 MERITAMUN, DAUGHTER OF RAMESSES II AND NEFERTARI, BECAME A GREAT ROYAL WIFE
(EGYPTIAN MUSEUM, CAIRO).

8 HEAD, IN VULTURE GUISE, SAID TO BE CLEOPATRA (CAPITOLINE MUSEUMS, ROME).

11 COLOSSUS OF HATSHEPSUT FROM THE DEIR AL-BAHARI TEMPLE (EGYPTIAN MUSEUM, CAIRO).

12-13 ANKHESENAMUN AND TUTANKHAMUN SHOWN ON A TABERNACLE (EGYPTIAN MUSEUM, CAIRO).

14-15 THE BURIAL CHAMBER IN THE TOMB OF NEFERTARI.

CONTENTS

WHITE STAR PUBLISHERS

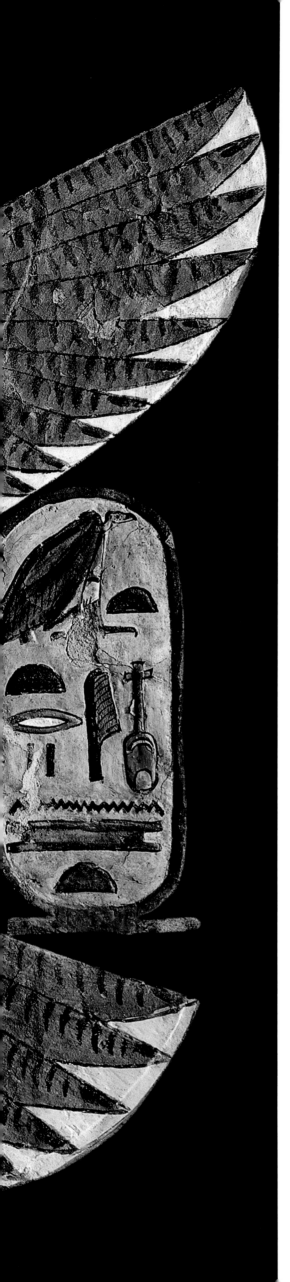

INTRODUCTION

THIS BOOK IS A CELEBRATION OF ANCIENT EGYPT'S IDEAL
OF FEMALE BEAUTY.

She looks like the rising morning star
At the start of a happy year.
Shining bright, fair of skin,
Lovely the looks of her eyes,
Sweet the speech of her lips,
She has not a word too much.
Upright neck, shining breast,
Hair true lapis lazuli;
Arms surpassing gold,
Fingers like lotus buds.
Heavy thighs, narrow waist, her legs parade her beauty.
With graceful step she treads the ground,
Captures my heart by her movements.

(Papyrus Chester Beatty 1, translation by Miriam Lichtheim, *Ancient Egyptian
Literature*, vol. II: *The New Kingdom*, Los Angeles 1976, p. 182)

Admirers of ancient Egypt have always been proud of the relatively high
status of women in Egyptian culture. Indeed, according to ancient Egyptian
law, women were more or less equal to men. They could own property and be-
queath it at will; they could be witnesses in court and obtain a divorce. In the
eyes of society, of course, women were still subject to their husbands or other
male members of the family. *The Teaching of Ptahhotep*, a Middle Kingdom
text, describes the woman's function in life succinctly as "a field good for her
lord" and, in giving the following advice to the future official, probably presents
a fairly accurate picture of her position in the family: "Love your wife with
proper ardor: fill her belly, clothe her back! Perfume is a restorative for her
limbs. Make her joyful as long as you live!" But it also cautions: "Remove her
from power, suppress her! . . . A female who is under her own control is rain-
water: when one enquires after her, she has flown away." The same text is also
more realistic about a woman's beauty, compared to the idealized description
in the poem above: "If you take to wife a plump woman, someone light-hearted, well known to her town, who is volatile, to whom the moment is fair, do not
reject her! Let her eat! The light-hearted woman provides fresh water." (Richard
Parkinson, *The Tale of Sinuhe and other Ancient Egyptian Poems 1940–1640
B.C.*, Oxford 1997, p. 257, 261).

16-17 THE POLYCHROMATIC IMAGE OF THE WINGED GODDESS MAAT, FROM THE TOMB OF
NEFERTARI (QV 66), PROTECTING THE CARTOUCHE WITH THE NAME OF THE QUEEN. THE GODDESS
HAS HER OWN EMBLEM IN HER HAIR: A PLUME THAT IS THE SYMBOL OF JUSTICE AND DIVINE LAW.

Texts, images, and archaeological evidence also offer some glimpses into the real life of Egyptian queens. Like all other women, they had to survive the hazards of childbearing (very great in the ancient world) as well as endure the frequent experience of the death of a young child. The queen of Punt was certainly not the only woman to have suffered a debilitating affliction. Bitterness about the hardships of life seems etched on the face of the elderly Queen Tiye, while Nefertiti - icon of female perfection - had to live with her husband's attachment to at least one other, albeit minor wife: the intriguing Queen Kiya. Pitiable aspects of queenly life in Egypt can be discerned in the burial goods of the three "minor" wives of Thutmosis III. These women bear Semitic names – Manhata, Maruta, and Manuwai – but among the hundreds of objects that remain from their funerary equipment only one single item, a nondescript glass vessel, is not Egyptian. Like Marie Antoinette, who was stripped of all the Austrian clothes with which she arrived in Paris upon her marriage to the French king (who at least shared the same Roman Catholic religion), the three foreign women sent to wed Thutmosis III left behind all traces of their origins and, on their deaths, were buried solely according to the customs of the host country.

Otherwise, beyond the bare facts of their existences, very little is known about the individual women who served as queens of Egypt. Perhaps the most personal words uttered by an Egyptian queen are to be found in a letter from one who is nameless. It was written at the end of the Amarna Period and addressed to the Hittite king and has (perhaps significantly) survived only in the Hittite, not the Egyptian, language: "My husband died," the queen wrote, "and I have no son. They say about you that you have many sons. You might give me one of your sons to become my husband. I would not wish to take one of my subjects as a husband." No record has survived concerning the Hittite prince who was sent to Egypt in response to this letter, nor do we know under what circumstances the queen lived. (Cyril Aldred, *Akhenaten, King of Egypt,* London 1988, p. 228).

Alongside this powerless outcry from a widow is the following text, which is the closest one is able to come to a personalized description of a royal woman's ascent to power. The text is crafted as a magnificent metaphor, likening Queen Hatshepsut's governance of the country as pharaoh to the handling of a ship on the Nile: "[Thutmosis II] ascended to heaven and united with the gods, while his son [Thutmosis III] stood in his place as king of the two lands, . . . and while his sister, the god's wife Hatshepsut, was conducting the affairs of the country, the two lands being in her care. With Egypt in obeisance she is served, the beneficent divine seed who has come forth before him (the king), the prowrope of Upper Egypt and mooring post of the southerners. She is the excellent sternrope of Lower Egypt, mistress of command, whose counsels are splendid, with whose words the two banks are pleased." (Peter F. Dorman, "The Early Reign of Thutmose III: An Unorthodox Mantle of Coregency" in Eric H. Cline and David O'Connor (eds.), *Thutmose III, A New Biography*, Ann Arbor 2006, p. 41). Later inscriptions reporting the deeds of Hatshepsut are for the most part highly political or politico-religious utterances, in which might be detected the progressive effacement of the individual woman behind the traditional role of male kingship. The same is true for painted and sculpted images. The public ones, in plain view for all to see, represented her as a man; only a few seated statues, which must have been placed in the interior chapels of her temple at Deir al-Bahari, depict her as the woman she was or at least hint at her female identity.

The real-life experiences or the individual personalities of Egyptian queens thus carry on an undercover existence in surviving texts and images. What these sources document in splendor are the various roles of the Egyptian queen: female counterpart to the pharaoh, incorporating one half of the "first pair" created by the sun god to be parents to all future gods and humans; mother of kings, worthy to be buried in her own pyramid beside her son and even revered, as was the case of Ahmes-Nefertari, the deified mother of Amenhotep I, the second king of the 18th Dynasty; priestess (and also occasionally incorporation) of predominantly female deities; God's Wife and Divine Adoratrice to Amun at Thebes; regent for an underage king; and, repeatedly, co-ruler with a pharaoh or even ruler in her own right.

Of course, in ancient Egypt the ruler was above all called upon to fill the role of a semi-divine mediator between the gods and the people, without much regard to his identity as a real, human person. Indeed, Erik Hornung has gone so far as to describe the Egyptians' understanding of history as the celebration of a sacred drama in which the pharaoh played the leading part. "Historical inscriptions and images from ancient Egypt," Hornung wrote, "do not narrate actual events. Instead they provide an entry into a solemn, ritualistic world that contains no chance or random elements." The Egyptian queen had a parallel role in this conception of royal life as a ritual performance, and the images illustrated in this book basically document such queenly performances, with little attention to chance or random elements that might reveal personal identity or record individual experience. Expressed through the medium of art, however, these images of beauty have the somewhat paradoxical effect of endowing the queens with an artistic, if not "real," individuality. No matter what Queen Nefertiti really looked like, what she felt, or who she was in her heart of hearts, her image is recognized today in virtually every country of the world. To an admittedly lesser degree the same is true of Queens Tiye, Ankhesenamun, Nefertari, Meritamun, or the queen known to us only from a single jasper fragment. In their statues, on their thrones, or among the plants of their gardens, these queens continue to live as enchanted - and enchanting - creatures to the present day.

Dorothea Arnold

CHAIRMAN OF THE DEPARTMENT OF EGYPTIAN ART
AT THE METROPOLITAN MUSEUM OF ART

WOMEN, QUEENS, AND GODDESSES IN ANCIENT EGYPT

CHAPTER 1

21 The polychromatic image is from the tomb of Menna (TT 69) and depicts his wife Henuttauy, Chantress of Amun. The woman's gaze is deep and seductive, and a main trait is her thick curly hair, partly pulled back to the nape of her neck and held in place by a lotus bud (a symbol of rebirth) floral band that tumbles onto her forehead.

22 This precious gilt bronze statuette portrays Isis as she suckles young Horus. If the latter is identified with the reigning pharaoh, the goddess can be equated to the mother of the king. As often happens, the suckled prince wears the so-called "blue crown" (Egyptian Museum, Cairo).

23 top Renenut, the "Lady of the Harvests," suckles the crown prince. The goddess is shown with a human body and the head of serpent, wearing the *shuty* crown. The image comes from the tomb of Khaemhat (TT 57), the royal scribe and inspector of the granaries in the north and south during the reign of Amenhotep III.

From its earliest history, the nature of Egyptian monarchy shows close bonds with the divine sphere. As early as the First Dynasty, two male (Horus and Seth) and two female deities, known as the "Two Ladies," were associated with sovereignty. The latter were Nekhbet, the vulture goddess of Upper Egypt, and Uto, the cobra goddess of Lower Egypt. During the Second Dynasty, however, the sovereign's cosmic role was explicitly associated for the first time with Maat, incarnating the concepts of law, order, and divine justice.

With the advent of the Heliopolitan theological system, which promoted worship of the sun god Re, one of the crucial elements of the Egyptian state, the sovereign was definitively established as divine offspring and regal titling was completed, so from the Fourth Dynasty the ruler was also called "Son of Re" (in Egyptian *sa-Re*). From this time onward the pharaoh was absorbed into the universality of the cosmos and associated with the sun god Re, as his son and heir. The god Re and his son Horus were flanked by a female deity, the cow goddess called Hathor, who was then identified as Re's wife and daughter, but also as the sovereign's wife and daughter.

The maternal role of Hathor or a female deity resembling her, was unequivocally expressed in the Fifth Dynasty's well-documented iconography showing the goddess suckling the young prince. The deity could be completely anthropomorphic and/or have a cow's head (as documented by the reliefs of Sahure and Niuserre in their burial complexes at Abusir or that of Seti I at Abydos); there are also completely zoomorphic examples, as in the case of the completely round sculpture with the name of Amenhotep II, placed in the chapel which Thutmosis III had dedicated to the goddess Hathor in the Deir al-Bahari sanctuary, now exhibited in the Museum of Egyptian Antiquities in Cairo (the Egyptian Museum). The identification of a goddess suckling as a central moment of the coronation ritual was suggested for the first time by the Egyptologist Jean Leclant and confirmed in the temple of Hatshepsut at Deir al-Bahari, where a suckling scene precedes that of robing the future monarch, when another goddess (Urethekau) gives the queen the insignia of regality and places herself on her forehead as a serpent-uraeus. When the robing was over the future sovereign would have to face purification, and then he could enter the intimate part of the temple to receive the laying on of the hands of the god Amun.

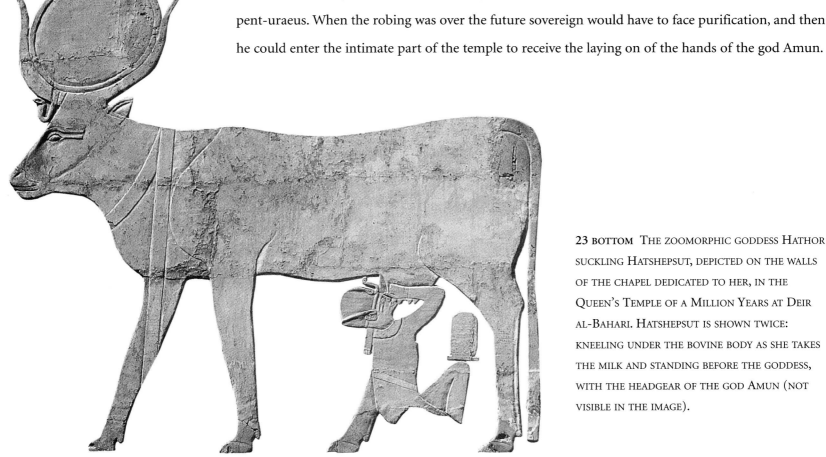

23 BOTTOM THE ZOOMORPHIC GODDESS HATHOR SUCKLING HATSHEPSUT, DEPICTED ON THE WALLS OF THE CHAPEL DEDICATED TO HER, IN THE QUEEN'S TEMPLE OF A MILLION YEARS AT DEIR AL-BAHARI. HATSHEPSUT IS SHOWN TWICE: KNEELING UNDER THE BOVINE BODY AS SHE TAKES THE MILK AND STANDING BEFORE THE GODDESS, WITH THE HEADGEAR OF THE GOD AMUN (NOT VISIBLE IN THE IMAGE).

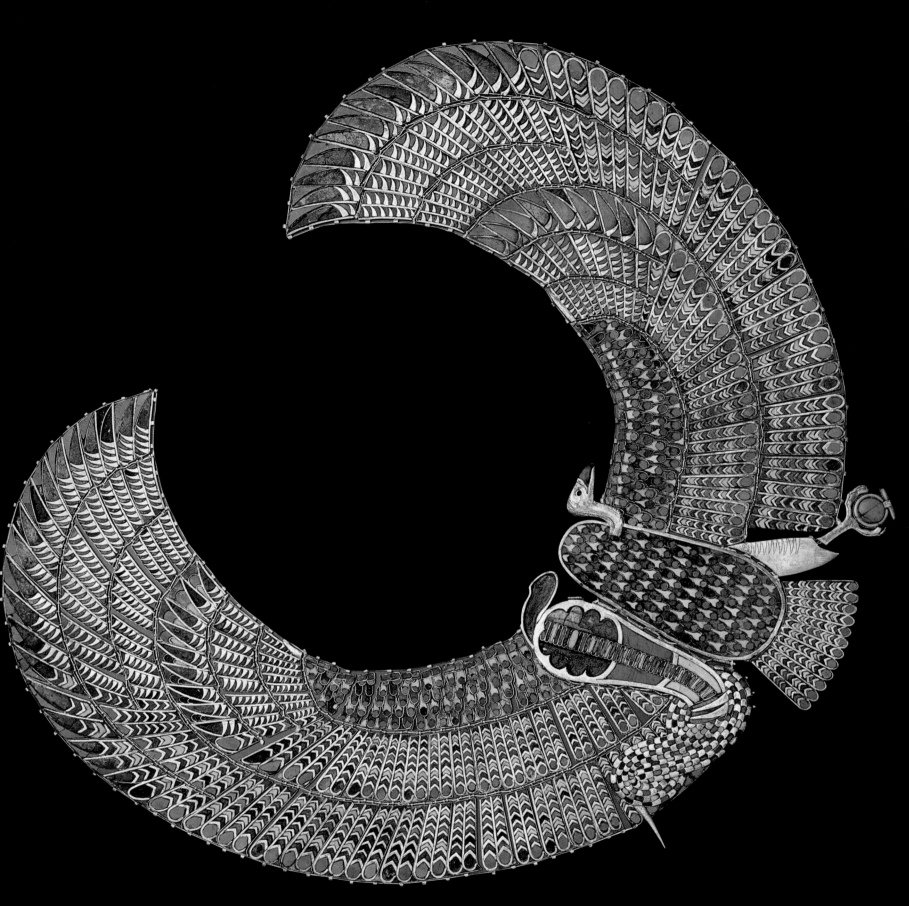

24 On one of the walls of the temple of Edfu, the goddess Uto of the North (left) and the goddess Nekhbet of the South (right) crown Ptolemy VIII (Evergetes II) with the double crown of Upper and Lower Egypt.

25 The multicolored gold and semiprecious stone collar is part of Tutankhamun's treasure and shows, flanked, the Two Ladies of Egypt: left, Uto, the serpent goddess of the North; right, Nekhbet, the vulture goddess of the South. The two divinities have been the protectors of the sovereign from the time of the earliest dynasties (Egyptian Museum, Cairo).

After being crowned, the Egyptian sovereign's main task was to maintain Maat, the concept around which the very essence of Egyptian civilization revolved at that time. The relationship between the pharaoh, the universal god, and Maat can be adequately summed up by the image of the New Kingdom, with the pharaoh kneeling before Amun-Re to endorse his role as King of Upper and Lower Egypt, offering the god an image of the goddess herself.

After the birth and coronation, the final two phases of the pharaoh's life cycle involved the royal jubilee (in Egyptian *Heb Sed*), celebrated usually during the thirtieth year of his reign, with the scope of regenerating the monarch's strength and allowing renewal of the cosmos, and the definitive leaving of earthly life, when he would become an Osiris and join the imperishable stars.

26 THIS GOLD AND LAPIS LAZULI AMULET DEPICTS THE GODDESS MAAT. THE HEAD IS SURMOUNTED BY A PLUME, HER EMBLEM AND THE SYMBOL OF JUSTICE, TRUTH, AND DIVINE LAW (EGYPTIAN MUSEUM, CAIRO).

27 RAMESSES II WEARS THE SO-CALLED BLUE CROWN AS HE OFFERS AMUN THE IMAGE OF MAAT; IN EXCHANGE, THE GOD GIVES HIM POWER AND VICTORY OVER HIS ENEMIES. THE BAS-RELIEF POLYCHROMATIC SCENE IS ETCHED INTO THE SMALL TEMPLE AT ABU SIMBEL.

28 THE GOLD PENDENT, PART OF TUTANKHAMUN'S TREASURE, DEPICTS THE GODDESS URETHEKAU IN HER SERPENT FORM, WITH HUMAN HEAD AND HANDS, SUCKLING THE YOUNG TUTANKHAMUN (EGYPTIAN MUSEUM, CAIRO).

29 TOP THE REPOUSSÉ GOLD AMULET REPRESENTS THE DOUBLE URAEUS. THE METICULOUS WORKMANSHIP HIGHLIGHTS THE COBRAS' ANATOMICAL DETAILS (EGYPTIAN MUSEUM, CAIRO).

29 BOTTOM THE TWO VULTURES REPRESENT THE COUNTERPART OF THE DOUBLE URAEUS AND DEPICT NEKHBET, THE WHITE GODDESS OF NEKHEN, THE SOUTHERN FEMALE DIVINITY THAT PROTECTS THE SOVEREIGN WITH HER AMPLE WINGS. THE AMULETS ARE CHARACTERIZED BY THEIR PAINSTAKING WORKMANSHIP, WHICH RENDERS THE DETAILS OF THE PLUMAGE, THE HEAD RESTING ON THE ARCHED NECK AND THE SHARP-CLAWED FEET (EGYPTIAN MUSEUM, CAIRO).

How does the female counterpart fit in with the pharaoh's life, cadenced by ritual? What is the queen's function in the constitution and maintenance of the monarchy? Above all, how does this role change, if it changes in substance, as time passes?

The debate around the role of women, and specifically the role of the pharaoh's wife in ancient Egypt focused, since the start of the last century, on a condition that shows an especially privileged female element in the society of the pharaohs compared to that seen in its contemporary or even in more recent societies.

One of the earliest elements that contributed to the establishment of this opinion – actually widely accepted – was the fact that the queens exercised the royal function with full authority since the earliest phases of Egyptian history.

Moreover, there was always also the female element's founding function in the establishment of sacred royalty, as well as a significant freedom and autonomy for common women in relations with men and in the management of their property, as emerges from juridical-administrative documents.

Sector studies, which recently involved numerous researchers in the context of human sciences, recently brought to light the particular role enjoyed by women in ancient Egyptian society, initiating a new series of studies on the topic. Details about the female world are to be found in the work of American author Lana Troy, *Patterns of Queenship in Egyptian Myth and History* (1986), dedicated to the divine and cosmogonic aspects of female royalty, as well as the full-scale study published by Gay Robins, *Women in Ancient Egypt* (1993), which in fact concentrates mainly on the condition of the common woman and dedicates the first two chapters to female royalty.

In Robins's opinion the Egyptian woman was far from being emancipated and was actually – and mainly – the prisoner of her reproductive role in a society governed chiefly by men. Although the condition of women in the elite and the royal family was clearly differentiated and judged as privileged compared to others, Robins tends, in any case, to downscale the space and the freedom of action allowed to many royal wives, especially in

the cases of wives of a lower rank or foreign princesses, some of whom were actually kept prisoner.

On the basis of these stimulating reflections, but without overlooking the great symbolic value of some expressions of Egyptian royalty, closely linked to the world of the divine and the laws that govern the cosmos, we will try to answer, at least in part, some of the questions arising from scientific discussion: can it be said that the Egyptian queen enjoyed a privileged status compared to other sovereigns in antiquity? If this was the case, did the centrality of her role depend on her relations with the pharaoh or on the fact that she incarnated the female counterpart of the divine element? Was her role primarily political or was it substantially cosmogonic? To this end, we will compare images and stories of queens from different eras, with images and stories of monarchs who were their contemporaries, using historical reconstruction based on written sources and on archaeological documentation, without leaving aside what has been handed down to us by mythological narration and other religious texts with regard to Egypt.

30 Sennefer, mayor of Thebes, who lived at the time of Amenhotep II and Thutmosis IV, is depicted with one of his wives, the royal wet nurse Senay.

31 Sennefer receives a cup from another wife, Merit, whose forehead is decorated with a lotus flower and who wears a large necklace.

32-33 The bas-relief scene comes from the mastaba tomb of Mehu (6th Dynasty) and shows rural activities. The three women, whose hair is held in a band, wear close-fitting white tunics and trinkets on their necks, arms, and ankles. They are shown winnowing corn.

33 These three wooden figurines are part of a group of statues of servants from the tomb of Niankhpepi the Black, at Meir. The three women have short hair, wear close-fitting tunics with a single shoulder strap and carry large baskets on their heads (Egyptian Museum, Cairo).

34 In this image Menna's wife, Henuttauy, a Chantress of Amun, is shown praying in the inner chamber of their tomb (TT 69).

35 The "hunt in the marshes" scenes are some of the most ancient in the repertoire of images that decorate private tombs in the Old Kingdom. The owner of the monument is shown in the act of hunting water birds and fish, together with members of his family. This scene comes from tomb TT 52, belonging to Nakht, Priest of the Hours, in the Temple of Amun, during the 18th Dynasty.

38-39 THE FOUR WOMEN MUSICIANS OF THE NEBAMUN BANQUET (TT 179) ARE RIGHTLY FAMOUS AS ONE OF THE MOST ORIGINAL WORKS OF 18TH-DYNASTY EGYPTIAN FIGURATIVE ART: THE GREAT VITALITY OF THE SCENE COMES FROM THE DIFFERENT POSITIONS IN WHICH THE WOMEN ARE SHOWN; THERE IS ALSO A UNIQUE USE OF PERSPECTIVE IN DEPICTING TWO OF THE MUSICIANS (BRITISH MUSEUM, LONDON).

40-41 Sennedjem and his wife are shown adoring various divinities (including Osiris and Ra-Harakhty) inside the burial chamber of their own tomb (TT 1).

41 top The women are the family of Pashedu, who lived during the reign of Seti I; they are portrayed in the act of praying on his tomb at Deir al-Medina (TT 3). The garb, makeup, and ornaments of these women are meticulous: worthy of note is the obvious use of nail varnish on fingers and toes.

41 bottom A group of female mourners greets the arrival of the deceased in his sarcophagus (shown in the upper register). The image is from the Theban tomb of vizier Ramose (TT 55).

WOMEN AS SOVEREIGNS

CHAPTER 2

THE QUEEN AND THE FEMALE DIVINITIES

The ancient Egyptian language did not have a specific and separate word to express the concept of "queen." Until at least the end of the Old Kingdom, a queen was referred to only by a number of titles and names that indicated her relationship (by direct kinship or acquired by marriage) to the pharaoh, who was considered both in his human persona and as a hypostasis of one of the male deities, chiefly Horus or Seth. The word "*nesuit,*" the feminine version of "*nesut*" (King of Upper Egypt), very rarely appeared from the Middle Kingdom onward, and was only used as an equivalent to the masculine term in lists, although it became more common in the Ptolemaic Age.

However, the titling of queens, besides indicating their relationship with the pharaoh, was also aimed at constantly associating the role of the king's wife or mother with that of certain female deities. By observing the names and privileges of several goddesses in the Egyptian pantheon (Isis, Hathor, Maat, Mut, Bast, Tefnut, Nekhbet, Uto, Urethekau, to mention a few), it is clear that their existence was primarily connected with the necessity of Egyptian philosophy to establish a manifold concept of the cosmic order. It is equally clear that they basically shared the same purpose of balancing the male element in the deity, in order to re-establish the unity of the primeval god in his dual capacity as creator and renovator, i.e., he who brings to life and regenerates. It is not surprising, therefore, to find that in religious texts, as well as on the walls of temples dedicated to religious worship or to the funerary cults of the sovereign, the same function could be fulfilled by different female deities, and even their names could be very similar.

The choice of one deity rather than another could depend on the historical moment, the location of the sanctuary or the cultural background that had produced a given religious text; but essentially the divine counterpart of the queen could be identified in two models, represented by the goddesses Isis and Hathor.

42 THE BAS-RELIEF OF NEFERTITI IN PROFILE WAS CARVED ACCORDING TO AMARNA ART PRINCIPLES (EGYPTIAN MUSEUM, CAIRO).

44 IN THIS DETAIL OF NEFERTARI'S TOMB (QV 66) WE CAN SEE THE QUEEN'S TITLES AND CARTOUCHE.

45 THIS DETAIL OF THE SEDAN CHAIR OF KHUFU'S MOTHER, QUEEN HETEPHERES, SHOWS PART OF HER TITLING: "MOTHER OF THE KING OF UPPER AND LOWER EGYPT" (EGYPTIAN MUSEUM, CAIRO).

46-47 Queen Nefertari is portrayed in the entrance to her tomb, playing *senet*, a game similar to modern-day checkers. In a burial context, the symbology was representative of the trials and difficulties the deceased would have to face in the afterlife to reach the kingdom of Osiris. The queen's titles and cartouche are shown opposite.

47 The cornelian ring bears the cartouches of Ramesses II (left) and Nefertari (right), facing each other. This, like many other documents of this period, shows without doubt this sovereign's desire to underscore the role of the Great Wife in the constitution of his own regality (The Louvre, Paris).

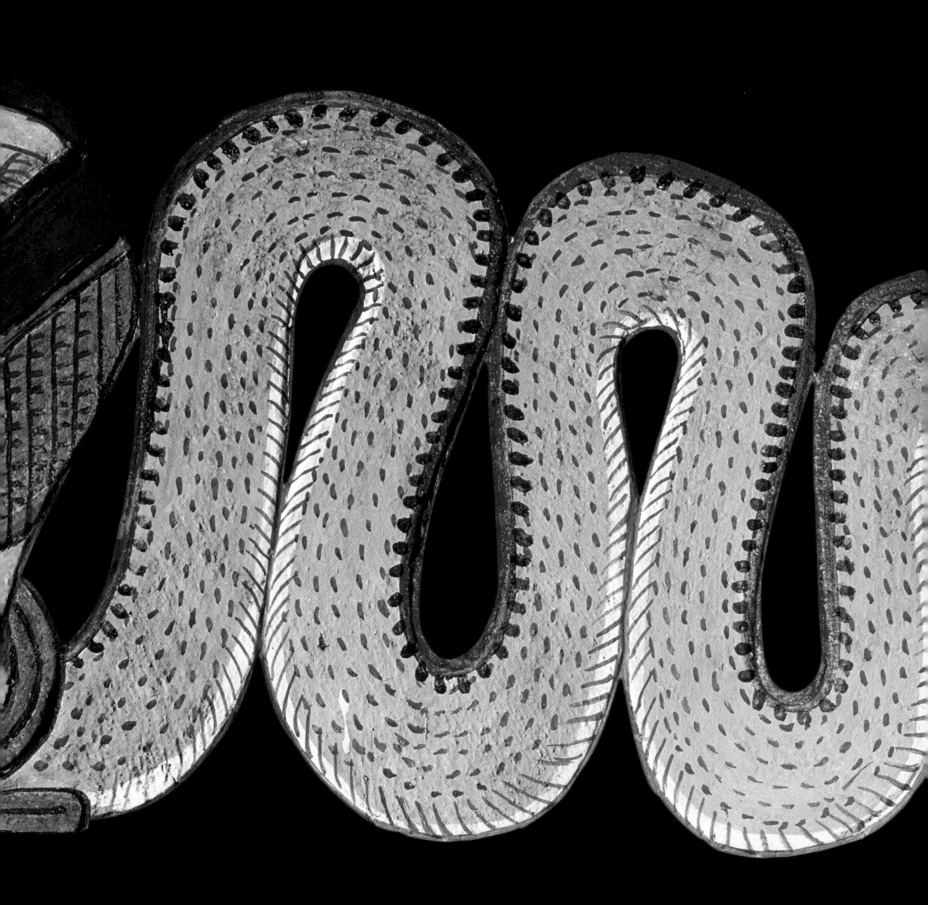

48-49 This divinity, in the guise of a winged cobra, resides in one of the triangular spaces created along the walls of a ramp leading down into the tomb of Nefertari, in the Valley of the Queens (QV 66). It protects one of Nefertari's cartouches.

ISIS AND THE CREATION OF THE EGYPTIAN STATE

One of the goddesses who best embodied the role of the Egyptian queen was Isis, wife and sister of Osiris. It is widely known that the most complete version of the myth of Osiris was handed down to us by Plutarch in his *De Iside et Osiride* at the beginning of the 2nd century AD. By comparing it with Egyptian religious texts, however, we may well claim that the content of Plutarch's version (although with a number of additions and variations) was based on an original written tradition, which referred partly to Pyramid Writings and collections of later funerary texts, such as the Sarcophagi Writings and the Book of the Dead, and partly to hymns and prayers dedicated to various deities. The myth describes the flourishing reign of Osiris, a divine king loved by his people and killed by his envious brother Seth, who dismembered his body and buried its pieces in various places around Egypt. Isis, the faithful wife and sister of Osiris, recovered his remains; thanks to her magic arts, she reconstructed his body and together they conceived a son, Horus, born after the death of Osiris. Then, with the help of a few male and female deities, she raised Horus by hiding him in the Chemnis swamps to prevent his uncle Seth from attacking him before he was ready to defend himself and avenge his father. When Horus came of age, he fought Seth and defeated him, thus taking his father's place on the throne of Egypt. From this myth not only do we learn a basic principle of Egyptian sovereignty, in which succession was vertical, from father to son, but we also notice the basic role of the royal wife, who acts as a guarantor not only for her partner's throne, but also for the legitimacy of his successor. In this regard, we must not forget that the divine symbol on the goddess Isis's head represented a throne, which is actually the hieroglyph used to write her name.

Finally, we must remember the special relationship between Isis and Osiris: not only were the two deities husband and wife, but also brother and sister. Since Osiris's family represented the primary model for a royal family, it comes as no surprise if Egyptian history hands down to us several cases of marriages between a pharaoh and his sister or stepsister, probably celebrated to solve dynastic issues.

50 THE GODDESS ISIS DEPICTED ON ONE OF THE PRECIOUS PECTORALS (A DETAIL IS SHOWN HERE) THAT IS PART OF THE TREASURE OF TUTANKHAMUN. THE KNEELING GODDESS STRETCHES OUT HER ARMS IN A GESTURE OF PROTECTION. ON HER HEAD, THE HIEROGLYPH OF A THRONE THAT IS USED TO REPRESENT HER NAME IN EGYPTIAN (EGYPTIAN MUSEUM, CAIRO).

51 RAMESSES III WELCOMED BY THE GODDESS ISIS, WHO GIVES HIM "THE LIFETIME OF RA." THE BAS-RELIEF IMAGE FROM THE TOMB OF PRINCE AMUNHERKHEPSHEF (QV 55) HAS LOST NONE OF ITS WONDERFUL COLORS.

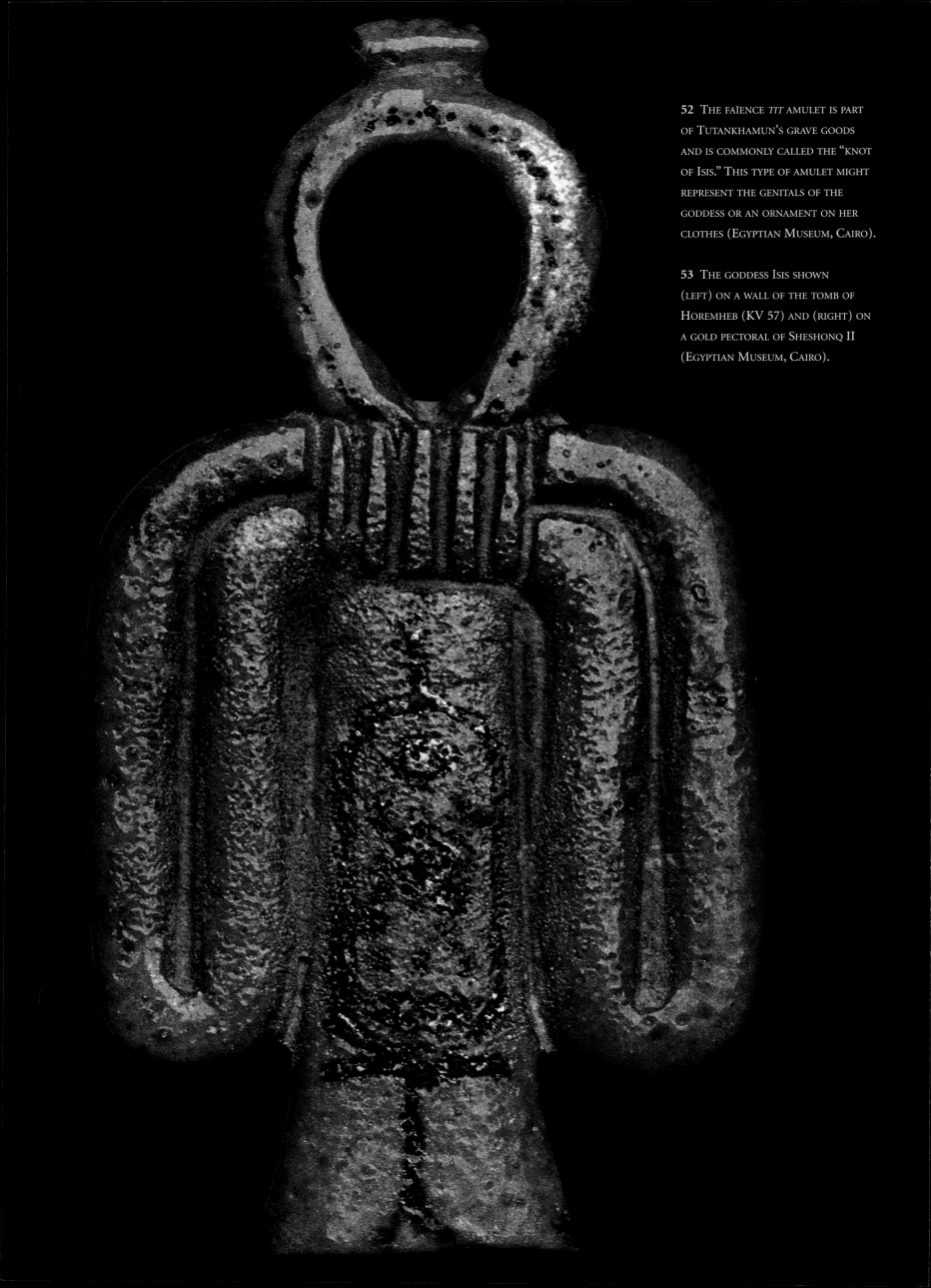

52 THE FAÏENCE *TIT* AMULET IS PART OF TUTANKHAMUN'S GRAVE GOODS AND IS COMMONLY CALLED THE "KNOT OF ISIS." THIS TYPE OF AMULET MIGHT REPRESENT THE GENITALS OF THE GODDESS OR AN ORNAMENT ON HER CLOTHES (EGYPTIAN MUSEUM, CAIRO).

53 THE GODDESS ISIS SHOWN (LEFT) ON A WALL OF THE TOMB OF HOREMHEB (KV 57) AND (RIGHT) ON A GOLD PECTORAL OF SHESHONQ II (EGYPTIAN MUSEUM, CAIRO).

HATHOR AND SOVEREIGNTY

From the Old Kingdom, the royal family had to conform to another divine model: the triad formed by Re, Horus, and Hathor, the cow goddess. The importance of this goddess is testified not only by the several statues that depict her in sculpted groups together with the sovereign, but also by her aforesaid role of mother who suckled the prince, so as to pass her divine essence on to him and prepare him for his royal duties. Moreover, Hathor was associated with the cobra goddess Uadjet, the dangerous fiery "eye of Re" who protected the pharaoh by placing herself on his forehead and becoming the quintessential symbol of Egyptian royalty. From the earliest history of the pharaohs, the titling of queens showed that the bond with this goddess was a fundamental element in defining their role, and this bond was kept alive by titling of priests throughout the Middle Kingdom. From the start of the New Kingdom not only was the identification of Hathor and the queen reiterated, but also represented one of the focal points in the new relationship then being established between humanity and deity. It was mainly with reference to the sovereign's wife that the bond between Hathor and the queen was consolidated, and there was almost confusion between the snake goddess and the royal wife. Identification between goddesses and queens was also expressed through a number of emblems, which either intensified or began to appear for the first time precisely during the 18th Dynasty: the former included the crown with two feathers or *shuti,* and later the double uraeus and a particular type of cobra called (by the scholar R. Preys) the "Hathor uraeus" (the typical royal snake, whose forehead is decorated, however, with the emblem of the goddess Hathor – a sun disk between horns) made its appearance. While the double uraeus and the two feathers immediately evoke the two eyes of Re and the Egyptian universe's dualism, the symbols connected with the Hathor uraeus appear to be more particular. This appeared for the first time in the temple of Queen Hatshepsut, where it was present in many scenes and was used to form the cryptogram of the queen's coronation name, *Maat-ka-re.* This very cryptogram evokes another association between the pair sovereign – Hathor and the goddess Maat, another of Re's daughters, who is the embodiment of the notion of reciprocity that links the pharaoh to the gods. While Hathor embodied the uncontrollable, fertile, erotic element, Maat instead represented the legislative aspect of the laws that governed the relationship between humanity and deity.

54 THE GODDESS MEHET-URET REPRESENTS ONE OF THE MULTIPLE MANIFESTATIONS OF HATHOR, LADY OF THE WESTERN MOUNTAINS. THIS WOODEN SCULPTURE WAS FOUND IN THE TOMB OF TUTANKHAMUN, AND HAS BRONZE HORNS AND MOUNTED LAPIS LAZULI EYES (LUXOR MUSEUM).

55 THIS STATUE OF HATHOR, FROM THE PERIOD OF AMENHOTEP III, WAS DISCOVERED IN 1989, IN A CACHE IN THE LUXOR TEMPLE. THE GODDESS IS DEPICTED AS ANTHROPOMORPHIC AND SEATED WITH HER ARMS IN HER LAP; IN HER RIGHT HAND SHE HOLDS THE *ANKH*, SYMBOL OF LIFE (LUXOR MUSEUM).

56 This detail of one of the walls of the tomb of Horemheb (KV 57) shows Isis who, from the time of the New Kingdom, was frequently assimilated to the goddess Hathor.

57 The façades of the columns in the burial antechamber of Amenhotep II's tomb (KV 35) show the king receiving life from Hathor. The goddess is here defined as "She Who Resides in Thebes, Lady of the Heavens."

58 The gold and lapis lazuli pendent set with hardstone eyes, shows the head of Hathor in mixed form, with human face and heifer ears (22nd Dynasty). The goddess's head in this version is often used to decorate column capitals or objects of various types dedicated to her (Egyptian Museum, Cairo).

58-59 The refined bas-relief profile shows a female figure, the head decorated with a diadem of flowers. In her left hand the woman holds the necklace with a *menit* counterweight and sistrum, both connected to the worship of the goddess Hathor (Egyptian Museum, Cairo).

The Hathor uraeus was reintroduced many times over and used in royal iconography during the reign of Amenhotep III and with a few slight modifications even in his coronation name. However, the Hathor uraeus was mainly depicted in a series of images related to Amenhotep III's Jubilee celebration, which decorate the walls of the Theban tomb of Kheruef. In this private monument, the sovereign's *Sed* festival was symbolically associated with the sun cycle through a rather complex figurative project, in which the pharaoh is depicted during the different stages of his Jubilee accompanied by two female figures: his wife and queen, with her forehead decorated with the Hathor uraeus (an incarnation of Hathor), and the goddess Maat. In other words, the bond was re-established between the sun god Re (here represented by the sovereign) and his two daughters, Hathor and Maat.

Although the Hathor uraeus, which was still widely present in the first period of the reign of Amenhotep IV's reign (successor to Amenhotep III), disappeared in the following Amarna period, the identification of the queen with the two goddesses did not change, and became even stronger, as is widely shown by the distinguishing iconography and the prominent role she played in all ceremonies and scenes depicting cults. In some cases, Nefertiti was even depicted without the pharaoh, as further evidence of the strong symbolic component surrounding the female element in the context of regeneration of the royal function's sacredness, stronger in that period than at other times in Egyptian history.

During the ensuing 19th Dynasty another female figure was often characterized by the presence of the Hathor uraeus: this was Nefertari, wife of Ramesses II. On the other hand, the small temple at Abu Simbel, which the pharaoh dedicated to his wife, clearly shows an intended confusion or juxtaposition between the images of Nefertari and Hathor.

60 A PART OF THE FIGURATIVE CYCLE DECORATING THE TOMB OF KHERUEF (TT 192) IS DEDICATED TO THE JUBILEE FESTIVITIES OF AMENHOTEP III. HERE THE SOVEREIGN IS SEATED IN A *NAOS* WITH THE "GREAT ROYAL WIFE TIYE."

61 NEFERTARI IS DEPICTED IN THE SMALL TEMPLE AT ABU SIMBEL AS SHE PERFORMS CEREMONIES LINKED TO THE GODDESS HATHOR. IN HER LEFT HAND THE QUEEN HOLDS A BOUQUET OF FLOWERS AND IN HER RIGHT SHE BEARS THE SISTRUM. ON HER HEAD, THE VULTURE REMAINS AS WELL AS HORNS WITH SUN DISK AND FEATHERS.

Although the Hathor uraeus was often associated with other queens during the New Kingdom, it is worth noting that the aforesaid reigns of Amenhotep III, Amenhotep IV, and Ramesses II shared another rather significant phenomenon: there are records for all three that at some point during their reigns these pharaohs married their own daughters, some of whom were titled Great Royal Wives. The nature of these marriages has been the subject of lengthy discussion, and there is no agreement on the two different interpretations: the most popular interprets them as dynastic or ritual matrimonies, whereas the other claims it is our moral attitude that prevents us from accepting the idea of real marriages between father and daughter.

It is worth mentioning other aspects of the reigns of these three monarchs, to shed more light on the matter and attempt to provide a more convincing interpretation of this phenomenon:

(1) during the last part of Amenhotep III's reign, four princesses had the title of royal wives, but only Sitamun, the daughter of the sovereign by Tiye, his first queen, was known as Great Royal Wife;

(2) during the second half of Amenhotep IV's reign, one of his daughters, Meritaten, assumed the title of Great Royal Wife as had Nefertiti; however, we cannot state with certainty whether the two queens shared the title at the same time, or whether Nefertiti was already dead at the time, since documents unfortunately became scarcer and, above all, less clear after the twelfth year of the reign;

(3) during Ramesses II's reign, at least six queens (four of whom were the sovereign's daughters) bore the title of Great Royal Wife: in the first part of the reign Nefertari was a great wife together with Istnofret, then Bintanat shared the title with Meritamun, and finally Nebettawi assumed the title with Henutmire.

So, at a certain point during their reigns and contrary to tradition, each of these kings associated two Great Royal Wives with their own figure. How can we interpret such an inconsistency?

64 The small, unfinished sculpture group depicts the pharaoh
Akhenaten, who kisses one of his daughters seated in his lap.
Intimate scenes of the family and love of offspring is an original
feature of Amarna art (Egyptian Museum, Cairo).

65 The head is an image of one of the Amarnian princesses, depicted
in the iconography that, in this period, often characterized figures
of the royal family, both in the two-dimensional representation
and in the round sculptures: the face, with its great almond-
shaped eyes, long nose and full mouth, ends in an extremely
elongated bald cranium (Egyptian Museum, Cairo).

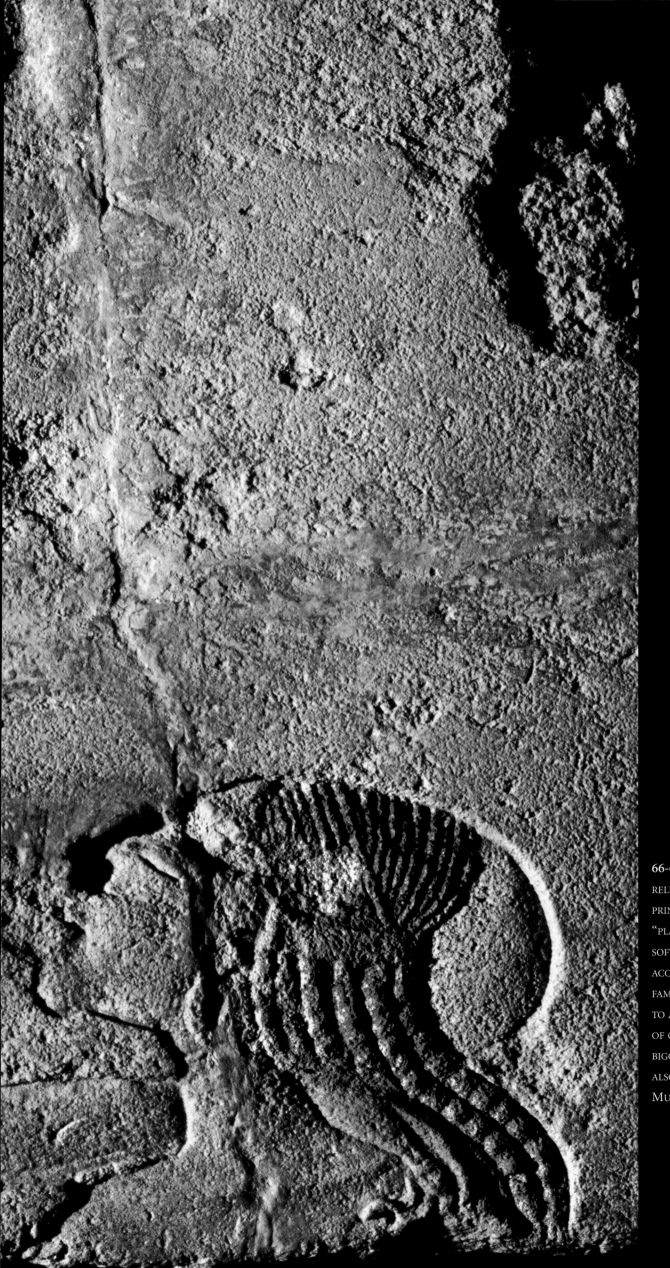

66-67 The polychromatic bas-relief shows two Amarnian princesses, both with the typical "plait of childhood." The softness of the gestures is accompanied by an attitude of family intimacy that is peculiar to Amarna art. The perspective of one of the breasts of the bigger of the two princesses is also unusual (Metropolitan Museum of Art, New York).

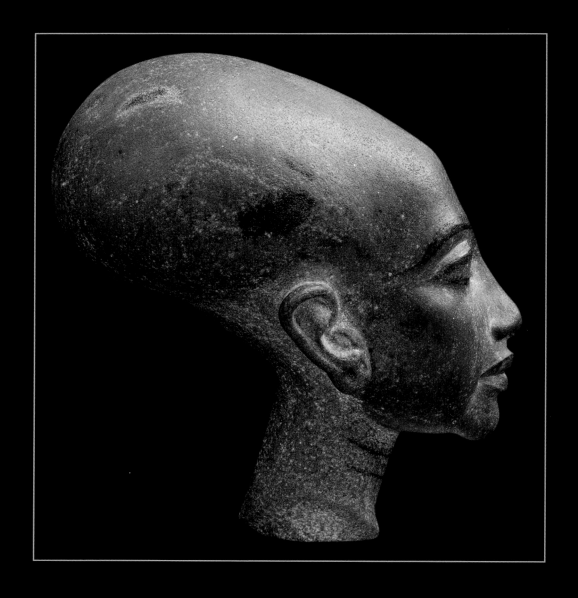

68 AND 69 THIS AMARNIAN HEAD WAS DISCOVERED,
WITH NUMEROUS OTHER STATUES, IN THE WORKSHOP
OF THE SCULPTOR THUTMOSIS, AT AKHETATEN, THE
NEW CAPITAL FOUNDED BY THE "HERETIC" PHARAOH,
AMENHOTEP IV/AKHENATEN. THE PROFILE VIEW
EMPHASIZES THE UNNATURAL LENGTH OF THE BALD
CRANIUM. THE FACIAL FEATURES AND THE EARS,
HOWEVER, ARE EXTREMELY NATURAL. THE EYEBROWS,
THE EYE AREA, AND TWO FINE CREASES IN THE NECK
ARE ALL PAINTED BLACK (EGYPTIAN MUSEUM, CAIRO).

In this respect, it may be useful to remember that another event marked the reigns of both Amenhotep III and Ramesses II, notwithstanding several differences: the process of deification while the sovereign lived, which both pharaohs achieved with great determination, the former starting from his first Jubilee, the latter even earlier, from the eighth year of his reign. Moreover, Ramesses II's decision to associate his own reign ideally with the 18th Dynasty's great ancestors, in particular with Amenhotep III, renders the analogies between the two kings even more evident.

If Amenhotep IV's deification is more controversial, and the nature of his relationship with the single god Aten appears to be more complex, nevertheless his reign was characterized by a program of religious policy aimed at showing the exclusive bond between the king, his whole family, and the solar deity, both through images and architectural constructions.

The very typology and the ways in which these three kings wished themselves and their royalty to be represented, permit a plausible interpretation of their decision to flank their own image not with one but two Great Royal Wives as an identification of their own nature with the very nature of the universal god. In other words, the two queens were supposed to fulfill the same functions as the divine couple of Hathor and Maat were called to perform alongside the Divine Creator. Notably, while the first Great Royal Wife took on the "political role," so she shared in the government of the country, the sovereign's daughter, in compliance with a religious concept dating back to the Old Kingdom and connected to the multiple role of Hathor, was identified with the daughter (though at the same time the mother) of Re, and was invested with the "cosmogony role": her task was to assure continuity to the cosmos and to its direct emanation, which was royalty. On these grounds, we may reasonably exclude both the idea that marriages between fathers and daughters were strictly speaking dynastic marriages aimed at ensuring an heir to the throne and continuity to the ruling family, and the idea that they were actually incestuous relationships between the sovereign and his daughters. The purpose of such explicitly promoted unions surely was that of reaffirming the sacredness of the royal function through the transposition of divine privileges to the pharaoh and his family.

THE TITLING OF THE QUEENS
AND THEIR RELATIONSHIP WITH THE PHARAOH

As already explained, the position of a woman within the royal family was defined by standard terms of kinship: Royal Wife, Mother of the King, Mother of the King's Children, Daughter or Sister of the King.

The first two titles in particular made up the very essence of a queen and her role: the first one indicated the Royal Wife as Isis, namely "she who guarantees the king the government of the country," and therefore invested her with an extremely important political role; the second one identified the queen as "she who gave birth to the new Horus" (the pharaoh), and of course was even more significant. Actually, while the pharaoh always had more than one wife, the position of the mother of the new king was inevitably unique so represented a central element of her figure and was reflected in the titling. As a matter of fact, in ancient Egypt, some Mothers of the King were also known as "Daughters of the God." The fact that this title did not express direct descent from the pharaoh as a god is shown by the fact that of six queens of Ancient Egypt who carried this title, only two had proven royal origins. Today the title of Daughter of the God is unanimously interpreted as a name connecting the queen with the goddess Hathor in her role as Daughter of the God Re, that is to say "she who renders possible the regeneration of the father." On the other hand, being identified with Hathor also meant playing the role of the goddess who was wet nurse to the sovereign-to-be, which was well suited to the Mother of the King.

It should be made clear, though, that this title was given to a queen only after her son had come to the throne and not to the mother of a prospective heir: in other words, it played no role at all in singling out the legitimate heir. The alternation on the throne of various branches of the royal family during the Old Kingdom shows that lineage problems were anything but rare, although there is evidence that there must have been a certain hierarchy among the princesses themselves: just think for example of the title of Eldest Daughter of the King.

Then there is the question: what became of those Daughters of the King who did not become Royal Wives and Mothers? From an analysis of the titling of these princesses of Ancient Egypt, it has emerged that many of them took title Priestess of Hathor and eventually were likely to take their place at the queen's side, probably as her personal handmaidens.

74-75 The burial slab of Neferetiabet, a princess of the 4th Dynasty. Neferetiabet sits in front of a table of offerings, around which various products are depicted and listed; the right-hand edge of the slab includes a list of precious fabrics (The Louvre, Paris).

76-77 In this detail of the statue group depicting Djedefre and his wife, we see the simple tunic and the humility of the queen's pose, who is kneeling at the sovereign's feet (The Louvre, Paris).

During the Middle Kingdom a significant series of changes in titling, as well as in iconography, bears witness to the intention of entrusting the queen with a rather important political role. Titles such as Lady of the Two Lands or Lady of All Lands no longer connected the Royal Wife with her own husband only, but also with all Egyptian territory, including foreign lands. The creation of such new privileges is confirmed by the consolidated use of the uraeus in an iconographic context and in the context of epigraphs by the introduction of the cartouche in the queen's name.

The title of Priestess of Hathor, which for some time no longer designated the daughters of the king, but rather his Royal Wives, and the subsequent name She Who is United with the White Crown, continued to highlight the bond between the queen and the goddess Hathor. Also during the Middle Kingdom, all the women belonging to the Royal Family, whether married or not, became commonly referred to as *iri-pat*, usually translated as "princess," though better rendered with "belonging to the elite" or "noble."

As was the case in the Old Kingdom, during the Middle Kingdom the titling of the king's unmarried daughters was extremely concise, because they had no specific role in maintaining the kingship. However, great prominence was given to all the women of the royal family, as can be inferred from the very rich female tombs in royal necropolises. The kings of this period seemed to be surrounding themselves with extremely numerous harems, with the obvious purpose of providing a large number of possible heirs.

However, it is worth pointing out that these harems could be a source of political instability. This is probably another reason why the kings of the Middle Kingdom tried to secure their succession further by quite regularly resorting to "co-regency," which allowed them to appoint their own heir, associating him with the throne at a certain point during their reign. Nonetheless, literary sources such as the renowned *Tale of Sinuhe* show that not even this solution was void of difficulties. Actually, the first part of the "novel" narrates how the ruler, King Amenemhet I, was killed by a plot hatched in his own harem, whose members then tried to foster a different prince from the one he had designated.

80-81 THE SMALL WOODEN HEAD, FOUND NEAR
AMENEMHET I'S PYRAMID AT LISHT, IS OF A YOUNG
WOMAN WITH AN AMPLE AND ELABORATE WIG,
PARTIALLY COATED WITH GOLD LEAF. THE WIG WAS
ATTACHED TO THE HEAD WITH TENONS. THE FACE HAS
REFINED FEATURES BUT HAS SADLY LOST THE MOUNTED
EYES (EGYPTIAN MUSEUM, CAIRO).

81 THIS ELEGANT SILVER MIRROR BELONGED TO
SATHATHORIUNET, DAUGHTER OF SENUSRET II, AND IS
SET ON AN OBSIDIAN HANDLE, TRIMMED WITH GOLD
AND HARDSTONES. THE HANDLE IS FORGED LIKE A
PAPYRUS STEM AND THE TIP IS A HATHORIC CAPITAL
(EGYPTIAN MUSEUM, CAIRO).

From the beginning of the New Kingdom, the new title of Great Royal Wife – attested for the first time during the Kingdom of Senusret III, and documented two or three times during the 13th Dynasty – became one of the most recurrent titles for queens, together with a new sacerdotal title, that of God's Wife (of Amun). In that era Amun had become a universal god (in his syncretistic form of Amun-Re), and the greatest monumental complex in Egypt, the Temple of Karnak, was dedicated to him. At the beginning of the 18th Dynasty, Queen Ahmes-Nefertari had a stele placed inside this sanctuary to bear witness to the establishment of the God's Wives order of priestesses. The recruitment procedure for these priestesses is still not absolutely clear; in most cases they were young women from the royal family, though more than one exception to this rule is known.

The purpose of the title and how it was connected to those of Great Royal Wife and Mother of the King is a long-discussed and as yet unsolved issue that deserves some consideration.

For instance, examining the titling of the queens during the first half of the 18th Dynasty in relation to the abovementioned titles, we see that the wife of the pharaoh could be: (a) God's Wife and Great Royal Wife; (b) only Great Royal Wife; or (c) only Royal Wife. Only in the first case did the queen almost always belong to the royal family, though this was not a prerequisite to become Mother of the King. Actually, during the New Kingdom, the number of queens and mothers of the king who were not of royal origin was very high.

Then we might consider the fact that one of the basic elements in royalty was the pharaoh's divine descent, guaranteed by his bond with the Universal god; this bond was expressed in the royal titling by the name Son of Re, as well as symbolically reaffirmed, just before his coming to the throne, through his being suckled by a female deity whose role was entrusted to the queen. On the other hand, we have already seen that both in the Old and the Middle Kingdoms there seems to have existed no clear hierarchy among the king's wives, and this must have caused various problems in dynastic succession.

82 The statue in painted wood was made during the reign of Ramesses II and depicts Ahmes-Nefertari, mother of Amenhotep I, deified with him and worshipped in the necropolis of Thebes (The Louvre, Paris).

83 Queen Ahmes-Nefertari is portrayed in this painting from a tomb of the 20th Dynasty, in Thebes, and of which the queen was patron of the necropolis together with her son Amenhotep I. The queen's skin is black and this refers to her Osirization (British Museum, London).

84-85 Ahmes-Nefertari and her son Amenhotep I are shown in front of a table of offerings; the two deified sovereigns are protected by the SA symbol and by a vulture goddess. The figures are carved into the wooden wall of a litter or a throne (Egyptian Museum, Turin).

The creation of the title Great Royal Wife should have partly settled the matter, since if the queen thus designated gave birth to a son, she would automatically become mother of the heir to the throne, assuming the role of Isis or Hathor. If, on the other hand, the Great Royal Wife only gave birth to daughters, then would a secondary wife, although of non-aristocratic origins, have assumed that same role?

Indeed, considering the last point, we may suppose that in the event that the king had no sons with his Great Royal Wife, a son of his born from a lower-rank wife would only come to the throne only after having married a God's Wife of Amun, thus recreating that direct bond with the god, to assure that his own nature was divine and to assure Egypt the new king was legitimate.

Not even this last tradition managed to avoid dynastic problems, and this is clearly shown by two cases: (a) the succession of Amenhotep I, who died young and without heirs; after his death, Thutmosis I, whose direct relation to the royal family is still controversial, came to the throne. We know his mother's name, Seniseneb, but very little can be said of his father: some scholars have hypothesized this could have been Ahmose Sipairi (probably the son of Tao II, one of the last princes in the 17th Dynasty); some others believe he was simply his predecessor's "right-hand man;" and (b) during the 18th Dynasty, the events characterizing the joint kingdoms of Hatshepsut and Thutmosis III; after a first phase of regency by Hatshepsut, a co-regency followed, in which the figure of Thutmosis III appears to have been altogether secondary to that of the queen; only after Hatshepsut's death was Thutmosis alone on the throne of Egypt, where he then ruled with full powers for over thirty years.

From the middle of the 18th Dynasty, the title of God's Wife of Amun was sometimes replaced by the title Divine Adoratrice of Amun, both in hieratic documents and in the titling of functionaries; it was replaced for good from the 20th Dynasty onward.

88 As can be read in the inscription, this statue is dedicated to Thutmosis III and his mother Aset, a secondary wife of Thutmosis II. The queen, seated on a chair with a low back, is wearing a close-fitting tunic with two straps and an elaborate *usekh* necklace (Egyptian Museum, Cairo).

89 This detail of the inner sarcophagus of Ahmes-Meritamun shows a face with delicate features framed by an ample Hathoric wig, the forehead decorated with a uraeus with sun disk (Egyptian Museum, Cairo).

90 THIS COLOSSAL SCULPTED GROUP PORTRAYS AMENHOTEP III WITH HIS WIFE TIYE AND THEIR THREE
DAUGHTERS. THE GREAT IMPORTANCE GIVEN TO THE ROLE OF THE GREAT ROYAL WIFE IN THE NEW
KINGDOM IS UNDERSCORED BY THE SIZE OF THE QUEEN, OFTEN PORTRAYED ON THE SAME SCALE AS THE
KING, AS IS THE CASE HERE (EGYPTIAN MUSEUM, CAIRO).

91 THE SCULPTED GROUP, FROM THE TEMPLE OF AMUN-RE IN KARNAK, SHOWS THUTMOSIS IV WITH
HIS MOTHER TIA. THE TWO SOVEREIGNS ARE SEATED NEXT TO ONE ANOTHER ON ONE SEAT; THEIR BOND
IS FURTHER EMPHASIZED BY THEIR FOLDED ARMS (EGYPTIAN MUSEUM, CAIRO).

From the Third Intermediate Period in particular, the figure of the Divine Adoratrice started changing substantially: her role was then fulfilled by a princess, the daughter or sister of the king, who devoted her whole life to the cult of the god Amun of Thebes, after having taken a vow of spinsterhood; her names (The Hand of God or She Who is United with the God) clearly describe her cosmogonic function, namely that of enabling the regeneration of the universe through her exclusive union with the Universal god. Her political function was nonetheless just as significant, at a time when only one part of the country was ruled by a royal dynasty and Thebes was under the control of the Priests of Amun. These priestesses, who were linked to the pharaoh, probably had to counterbalance the absolute power of the clergy in favor of the ruling family. Since she could not marry, the Divine Adoratrice appointed her successor by adopting her. Throughout the Third Intermediate Period, the Divine Adoratrices replaced the Royal Wife – whose role appeared to have disappeared gradually – both in her political and cosmic functions.

92 The black granite sphinx with female head and human hands, represents the Divine Adoratrice Shepenupet offering a vase with the head of a ram, an animal sacred to the god Amun. The princess was a daughter of King Pi(ankhi) and wears a Hathoric wig (Egyptian Museum, Berlin).

93 The tablet case is in nielloed bronze, with gold and silver inlays: it belonged to the Divine Adoratrice Shepenupet II, daughter of King Pi(ankhi). The upper part is etched with a starry sky and a series of symbols of protection, whereas the lower part is occupied by a prayer for Shepenupet, dedicated to her by Hor, Chief Scribe and personal secretary (The Louvre, Paris).

THE ICONOGRAPHY OF THE QUEENS

From what has been said so far, it seems evident that the centrality of the role of the King's Wife and of his Mother, both in royal symbols and as being responsible for ensuring an heir to the throne, had allowed the queens to share in the sacrality of the royal function. Nevertheless, in its most ancient stages their iconography had not diverged much from that of other women in the royal family. Basically, we can single out two types of iconography: images of queens represented in low relief on their own burial monuments, and those represented by in-the-round statues, chiefly sculpted in groups together with the king. In the former, their clothing essentially comprised a close-fitting tunic made of decorated material embellished with floral crowns and other kinds of jewelry and held up by shoulder straps, while their hair was often short. The in-the-round or high-relief sculptures, on the other hand, showed very simple women: their clothing usually consisted of a long close-fitting tunic tightly wrapped around their bodies like a girdle, without any ornaments; the wig was usually smooth, sometimes with streaks that showed the locks, with or without a middle parting. Contrary to what is shown in low relief, there is no evidence of jewels. The uraeus, seldom present in low relief, has never been reported for statues, with the only probable exception of the statuary group of Ankhnesmerire II with her son Pepi II on her lap.

There were no standard proportions or sizes for the uraeus: given the small number of examples, we can instead assert that they changed from one sculpture to another. Within groups they could greatly diverge between the king and the queen, or they could be absolutely identical. Finally, as regards internal proportions, all female figures, whether representing queens, goddesses or "ordinary women," were made to be the same as those of men: wide shoulders and chest, a narrow pelvis and a high waistline. Male and female facial features were very similar and were standardized with those of royal portraiture.

94 AND 95 THE SCULPTED GROUP (LEFT), FOUND IN THE GIZA TOMB, SHOWS HETEPHERES II, WITH HER ARM AROUND HER DAUGHTER MERSEANKH III (MUSEUM OF FINE ARTS, BOSTON). THE PAINTING (RIGHT) OF MERSEANKH III, GRANDDAUGHTER OF KHUFU AND WIFE OF KHAFRE, SHOWS HER WITH HER MOTHER HETEPHERES II, IN THEIR GIZA TOMB. THE OLDER QUEEN PRECEDES HER DAUGHTER AND IS IN THE OSIRIAN POSE, WHILE MERSEANKH IS PRESENTED AS THE FUNERAL PRIESTESS AND WEARS A PANTHER SKIN.

96 This extraordinary female statue is Nofret, wife of Rahotep, one of the sons of Snofru (Egyptian Museum, Cairo).

97 This sculpture shows Menkaure, probably with Khamerernebty II. The queen, in very simple garb, is depicted the same size as her husband (Museum of Fine Arts, Boston).

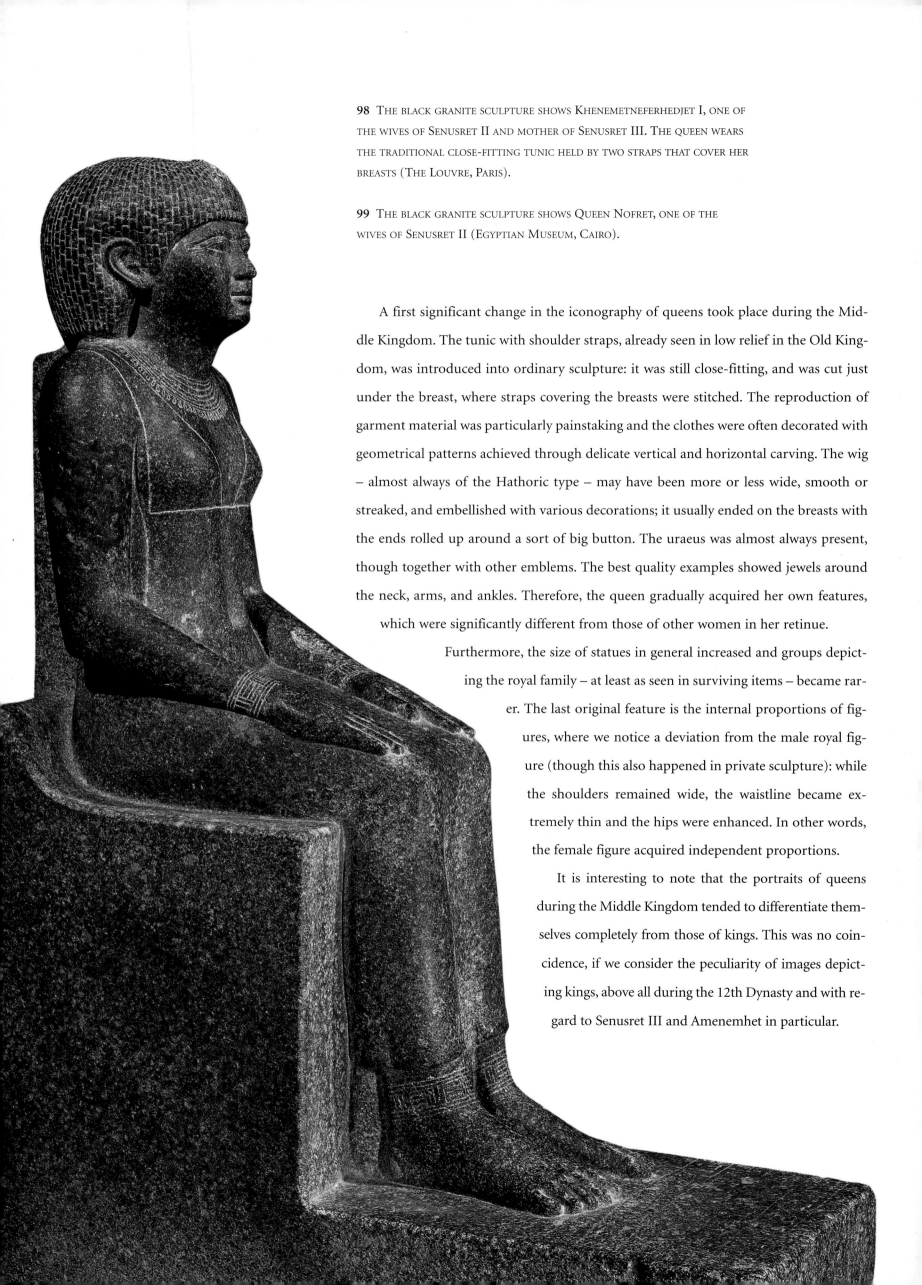

98 The black granite sculpture shows Khenemetneferhedjet I, one of the wives of Senusret II and mother of Senusret III. The queen wears the traditional close-fitting tunic held by two straps that cover her breasts (The Louvre, Paris).

99 The black granite sculpture shows Queen Nofret, one of the wives of Senusret II (Egyptian Museum, Cairo).

A first significant change in the iconography of queens took place during the Middle Kingdom. The tunic with shoulder straps, already seen in low relief in the Old Kingdom, was introduced into ordinary sculpture: it was still close-fitting, and was cut just under the breast, where straps covering the breasts were stitched. The reproduction of garment material was particularly painstaking and the clothes were often decorated with geometrical patterns achieved through delicate vertical and horizontal carving. The wig – almost always of the Hathoric type – may have been more or less wide, smooth or streaked, and embellished with various decorations; it usually ended on the breasts with the ends rolled up around a sort of big button. The uraeus was almost always present, though together with other emblems. The best quality examples showed jewels around the neck, arms, and ankles. Therefore, the queen gradually acquired her own features, which were significantly different from those of other women in her retinue.

Furthermore, the size of statues in general increased and groups depicting the royal family – at least as seen in surviving items – became rarer. The last original feature is the internal proportions of figures, where we notice a deviation from the male royal figure (though this also happened in private sculpture): while the shoulders remained wide, the waistline became extremely thin and the hips were enhanced. In other words, the female figure acquired independent proportions.

It is interesting to note that the portraits of queens during the Middle Kingdom tended to differentiate themselves completely from those of kings. This was no coincidence, if we consider the peculiarity of images depicting kings, above all during the 12th Dynasty and with regard to Senusret III and Amenemhet in particular.

100 This small sculpted group, in enameled schist, showed Amenhotep III (of whom only one arm remains) in the company of Tiye (The Louvre, Paris).

101 This detail of a scene painted on the tomb of Nefertari shows the queen's hand gripped in that of a female deity. The color contrast between Nefertari's skin (natural pink) and the golden yellow of the goddess's skin should be noted because the Egyptians believed that the bodies of the gods were forged from precious metal.

The changes in the iconography of queens that occurred during the New Kingdom allow us to assert the contrary of what we said with regard to the Old Kingdom. It was no longer possible to fail to distinguish the image of a queen from that of another woman in the royal family. On the contrary, from the point of view of their features, the faces of the queens became so standardized with those in the portraits of kings, that in some cases the two images in a sculpture group seem to have been superimposed.

Clothing was least affected by changes, at least until the Amarna period. During the first half of the 13th Dynasty, queens continued to wear the close-fitting tunic held up by shoulder straps covering the breasts, and often decorated with rosettes. An interesting variation is documented, for instance, by a glazed-stone statuette (Louvre Museum) representing Queen Tiye, wife of Amenhotep III, wrapped up in a tight-fitting tunic decorated with the wings of the vulture goddess, which seem to be embracing the sovereign's body. Starting from the second half of the dynasty, clothes became more varied: rich gathering appeared, as well as soft draping that cloaked queens and princesses. This new style was not completely given up even after the post-Amarna restoration; as a matter of fact, while queens depicted by in-the-round sculptures went back to pre-Amarna fashion, private statues and male royal sculptures maintained the use of stiffer draping, which was used for queens in low relief and paintings.

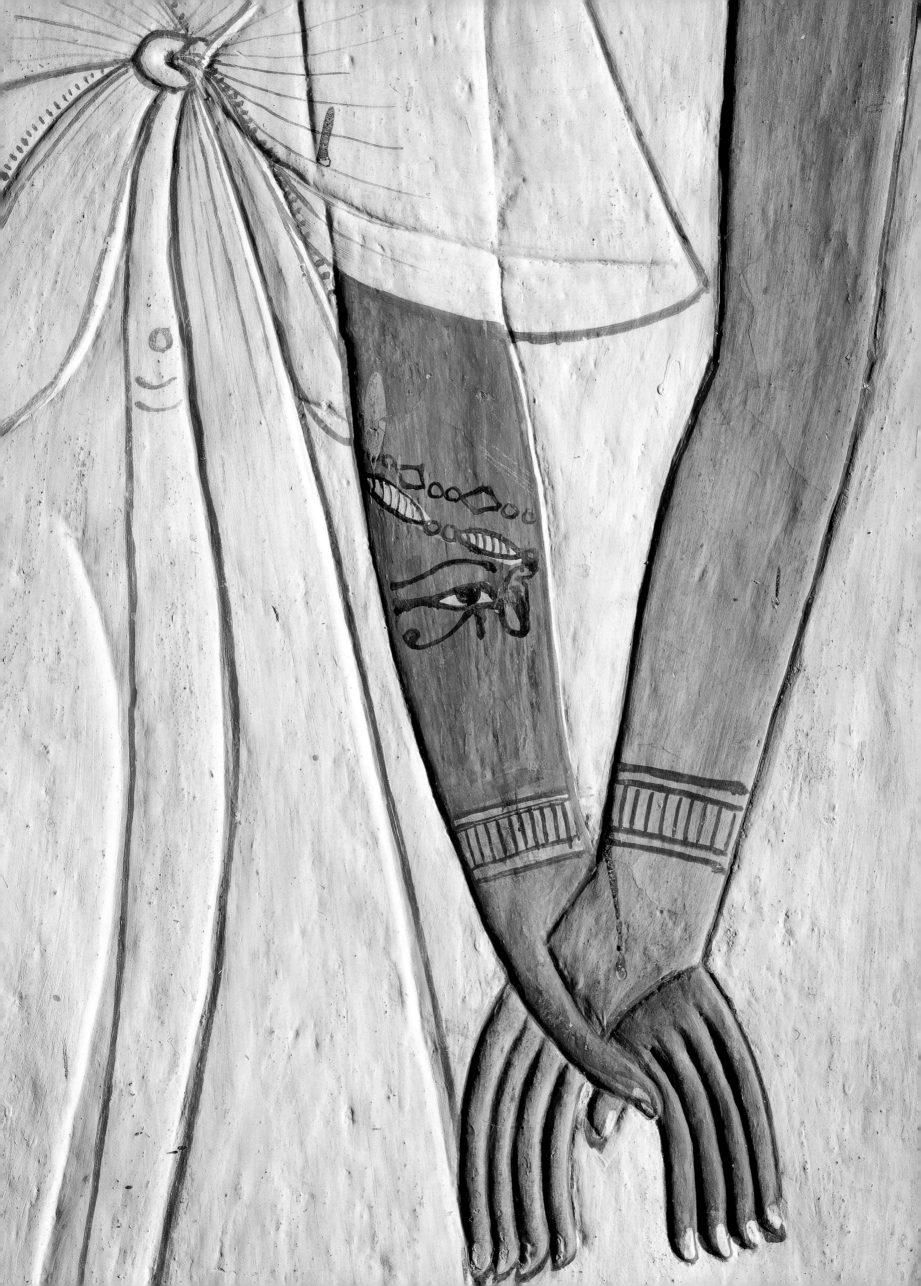

However, the greatest changes in the New Kingdom mainly concerned the queens' wigs and headdresses, enriched with a whole series of emblems that had previously been reserved for deities. These were the most popular models:

(1) the Hathoric wig, with straight or flicked-up ends as in the Middle Kingdom, still decorated with a vulture's head (symbol of the goddess Nekhbet);

(2) a rather stiff three-fold wig, heavily framing the face, and on which the locks were variously rendered with more or less deep carving on the surface. It was often surmounted by a diadem of uraei with sun disk, formed by a sun disk and/or a double feather. Contrary to the Hathoric wig, the three-fold wig did not always feature the vulture's head;

(3) a third type of wig very frequently used in the Amarna period recovered the wide short crown dating back to the Old Kingdom; and

(4) there was also vaguely cylindrical headgear in the Amarna period: it was typical of princesses and was always worn by Nefertiti.

The queen's forehead was always decorated with the uraeus, often double and/or flanked by a vulture's head.

The use of the symbols of the Two Ladies, the vulture goddess Nekhbet from the South and the snake goddess Uto from the North, explicitly recalls sovereignty over Upper and Lower Egypt.

As for jewels, no substantial change is recorded compared to the Middle Kingdom.

104 AND 104-105 THE CANOPIC CALCITE VASE
FOUND IN THE TOMB KV 55 (AN AMARNIAN
HIDING PLACE) OF THE VALLEY OF THE KINGS,
TRANSPORTED THERE BY TUTANKHAMUN WHEN HE
ABANDONED THE TOWN OF AKHETATEN. THE
IDENTITY OF THE OWNER IS STILL UNKNOWN BUT
IT MUST CERTAINLY HAVE BEEN ONE OF THE
WOMEN OF THE ROYAL FAMILY, AS SHOWN BY THE
HOLE IN THE NUBIAN-STYLE WIG, WHERE THE
URAEUS WOULD HAVE BEEN HOUSED (EGYPTIAN
MUSEUM, CAIRO).

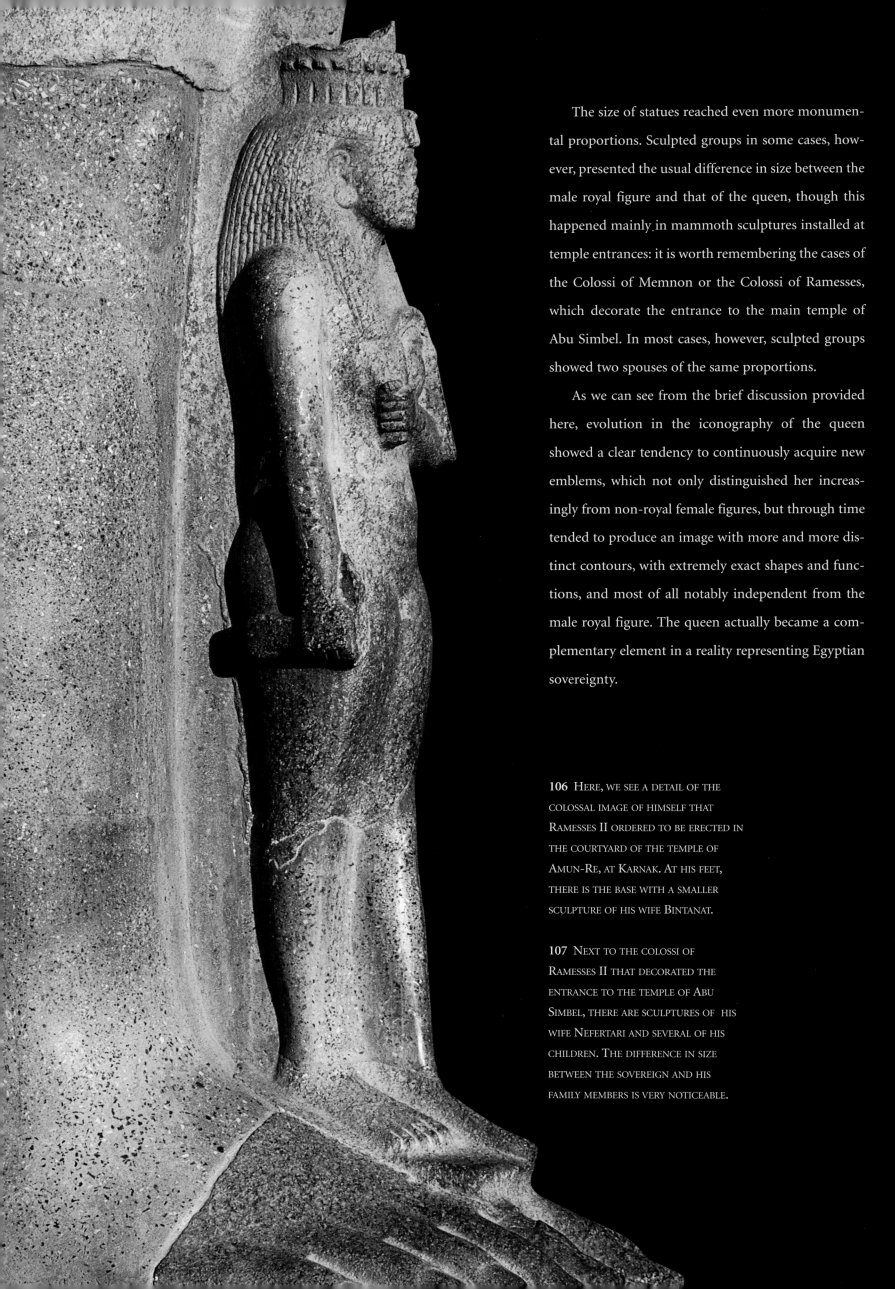

The size of statues reached even more monumental proportions. Sculpted groups in some cases, however, presented the usual difference in size between the male royal figure and that of the queen, though this happened mainly in mammoth sculptures installed at temple entrances: it is worth remembering the cases of the Colossi of Memnon or the Colossi of Ramesses, which decorate the entrance to the main temple of Abu Simbel. In most cases, however, sculpted groups showed two spouses of the same proportions.

As we can see from the brief discussion provided here, evolution in the iconography of the queen showed a clear tendency to continuously acquire new emblems, which not only distinguished her increasingly from non-royal female figures, but through time tended to produce an image with more and more distinct contours, with extremely exact shapes and functions, and most of all notably independent from the male royal figure. The queen actually became a complementary element in a reality representing Egyptian sovereignty.

106 HERE, WE SEE A DETAIL OF THE COLOSSAL IMAGE OF HIMSELF THAT RAMESSES II ORDERED TO BE ERECTED IN THE COURTYARD OF THE TEMPLE OF AMUN-RE, AT KARNAK. AT HIS FEET, THERE IS THE BASE WITH A SMALLER SCULPTURE OF HIS WIFE BINTANAT.

107 NEXT TO THE COLOSSI OF RAMESSES II THAT DECORATED THE ENTRANCE TO THE TEMPLE OF ABU SIMBEL, THERE ARE SCULPTURES OF HIS WIFE NEFERTARI AND SEVERAL OF HIS CHILDREN. THE DIFFERENCE IN SIZE BETWEEN THE SOVEREIGN AND HIS FAMILY MEMBERS IS VERY NOTICEABLE.

Finally, with regard to the Late Period, we have observed an almost complete absence of queens in the representation of sovereignty. Their function was entrusted to the Divine Adoratrices, whose portraits became uniform with those in female royal sculpture during the New Kingdom, although they also resumed very ancient iconographic elements, such as the extremely tight-fitting, body-wrapping tunic (possibly decorated with a vulture's wings). The wig could be of two sorts: (a) the long version with three folds, covered with a vulture's head and usually decorated with the double uraeus and with a small crown of uraei, on which either a double feather or horns with a sun disk were mounted; and (b) the short, streaked, slightly rounded version, surmounted by one of the described emblems. Wrists and ankles were decorated with jewels. A constant element in the iconography of the Divine Adoratrices was a kind of fan with a lily-shaped end, held in one hand, while the other could either hold the Hathoric sistrum or the *menit* necklace counterweight, itself connected with the cult of the goddess Hathor.

This type of iconography was later brought back into use by the Ptolemaic queens.

108-109 THE PRECIOUS SARCOPHAGUS OF THE
DIVINE ADORATRICE MAATKARE, DAUGHTER OF
PINUDJEM I, THE HIGH PRIEST OF AMUN (21ST
DYNASTY), WAS FOUND IN THE *CACHE* OF DEIR
AL-BAHARI (EGYPTIAN MUSEUM, CAIRO).

109 THE SCHIST STATUETTE DEPICTS THE DIVINE
ADORATRICE SHEPENUPET II, DAUGHTER OF
PI(ANKHI) (25TH DYNASTY). SHEPENUPET
SUCCEEDED AMENIRDIS I AND ADOPTED FIRST
AMENIRDIS II AND THEN NITOCRIS, DAUGHTER OF
PSAMMETICHUS I. SHE WAS BURIED AT MEDINET
HABU (EGYPTIAN MUSEUM, CAIRO).

THE QUEENS OF PHARAONIC EGYPT

CHAPTER 3

110 THE QUARTZITE HEAD OF A QUEEN OF THE
AMARNA PERIOD WAS FOUND IN THE MEMPHIS AREA
(EGYPTIAN MUSEUM, CAIRO).

112 HORUS, THE FALCON GOD, AND THE GODDESS ISIS
PERFORM RITUALS FOR THE RESURRECTION OF OSIRIS.
ON THE BODY OF THE ITHYPHALLIC GOD WE CAN READ:
"SOKARIS-OSIRIS WHO IS IN HIS BOAT." THE SCENE IS
SCULPTED IN BAS-RELIEF IN THE CHAPEL OF PTAH-
SOKARIS, WHICH IS IN SETI I'S TEMPLE AT ABYDOS.

112-113 THE GODDESS ISIS, FLOATING IN THE
LIKENESS OF AN EAGLE OVER OSIRIS' BODY, IS
FECUNDATED BY THE GOD. ON THE MUMMIFORM
BODY OF THE GOD WE CAN READ: "OSIRIS-
UNENNEFER WHO IS IN THE HOUSE OF SOKARIS,
GIVES LIFE AND POWER TO MENMAATRA (SETI I)."
THE SCENE IS SCULPTED IN BAS-RELIEF IN THE
CHAPEL OF PTAH-SOKARIS, WHICH IS IN SETI I'S
TEMPLE AT ABYDOS.

According to Manetho, an Egyptian priest who
Ptolemy II commissioned to write a history of Egypt,
from the 2nd Dynasty it was already possible by
Egyptian law for a woman to reign on the throne of
the pharaohs. The version handed down to us by the
myth of Osiris, seems to contradict this affirmation,
and in any case in the long period of pharaonic history, the number of queens who actually ruled in their
own right was very limited. At the same time, however,

such mythology paved the way for another custom, which was implemented on more than one occasion in the three millennia of Egyptian history: the regency exercised by the mother of an heir who was too young to reign.

However, even when the queen did not have the direct responsibility of ruling the country, but merely the role of supporting her own consort, the myths, on which regality and, as a consequence, the whole of Egypt were founded, made her a fundamental element in the cosmic balance and its regeneration.

It is probably for this reason that since the earliest dynasties, archaeological and textual documentation records a considerable number of important female figures. If there is some disparity in the documentation it is probable that this depends not so much (and not only) on the evolution of the role of female regality over time, but also on the objective difficulty in finding sufficient evidence on such an ancient period.

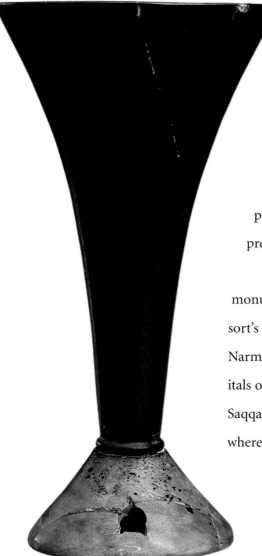

114 THE SCHIST GOBLET
WITH LIMESTONE SHANK WAS
PART OF HERINEITH'S GRAVE
GOODS. THE QUEEN WAS THE
WIFE OF DJER AND PROBABLY
THE MOTHER OF DJET:
SHE HAS BEEN ATTRIBUTED
WITH TOMB S 3507 AT
SAQQARA NORTH (EGYPTIAN
MUSEUM, CAIRO).

115 LEFT THE SEAL IMPRINT
FROM ABYDOS CONTAINS
THE NAMES OF SOVEREIGNS
FROM THE 1ST DYNASTY
AND ALSO MENTIONS
QUEEN MERINEITH.

True or false as Manetho's affirmation may be, it is a fact that some monuments and documents of the First Dynasty provide us with proof of the probable reign of a female sovereign, or at least the evidence of her very important political and ideological role: Queen Merineith, who was probably the wife of Djet, one of the dynasty's first kings, and mother of Den. Like other sovereigns from this period, Merineith has two regal tombs, one at Abydos (Tomb Y) in the south of Egypt and one in the Saqqara necropolis (3503) in the north.

The tombs at Abydos, built in the desert are relatively small and have a superstructure made up of a burial mound of crushed stone and sand, with a curved roof enclosed by slightly tilting brick walls. The Saqqara tombs, however, were more monumental (in some cases they were over 16 ft high/4.8 m) and their superstructure comprised entirely of raw brick. The walls were decorated in the characteristic palace façade style, constituted by a series of niches along the whole length, which was probably a replica of that of the royal palace.

Merineith's tomb in Abydos is one of the largest and best constructed of the royal necropolises of this period: the walls of the infrastructure are covered in raw bricks, with which eight small rooms – to house grave-goods – were also built around the funerary chamber. The ceiling and floor of the funerary chamber were made of wood. The materials included not only the documents indicating the names of three First Dynasty sovereigns, but also a funerary stele that is now in the Egyptian Museum in Cairo.

The monument, which is exactly the same as funerary stelae of sovereigns of the period, bears the queen's name but without the *serekh* (rectangular object that probably reproduces the façade of the royal palace and commonly contains the pharaoh's Horus name). The most plausible theory is that Merineith ruled as regent in her son Den's name. Moreover, her name is present on the Palermo Stone, where she is mentioned as the king's mother.

Merineith is not the only female figure among those documented by the royal funerary monuments of the Archaic Period: if queens usually had a funerary chamber inside their own consort's monument, there is more than one princely tomb belonging to a queen. Neithhotep, Narmer's wife, had a tomb with a palace façade in Naqada, one of the most ancient provincial capitals of pre-dynastic Egypt; Herineith, Djer's wife was in all probability the owner of tomb 3507 in Saqqara, while Shepsestipet, of the 2nd Dynasty, could be the owner of *mastaba* 3477 in Saqqara, where a stele with her name was found: the tomb contained the body of a woman aged about 60.

The end of the Archaic Period is marked by another queen, Nimaathapi, who is of great importance for the reconstruction of the transition phase between the 2nd and the 3rd Dynasties. Nimaathapi appears to have been Khasekhemui's wife (last king of the 2nd Dynasty) and mother of Djoser's mother (one of the first kings of the 3rd Dynasty). As well as being mentioned in contemporary documents, the queen was also the object of a posthumous cult, at the beginning of the 4th Dynasty, probably due to her link with a fundamental figure like that of Djoser. Two important new elements indeed characterize this sovereign's reign, which mark the beginning of the Old Kingdom: the use of stone only for the construction of royal funerary complexes and the building of the first pyramid, which became the symbol of the pharaohs from that moment onward and, for more than a thousand years, their burial place.

It was in fact in the Great Pyramid of Giza, that of Khufu (popularly called Cheops' Pyramid; second king of the 4th Dynasty), that an extraordinary discovery regarding another female figure was made in 1925.

The queens of this period were usually buried in small pyramids, built close to the tomb of their consort: by pure chance, on the eastern side of the Great Pyramid, the team led by the American Egyptologist, George Andrew Reisner, discovered the access to a tunnel that led to a ramp and then to a shaft. Filled with emotion, the archaeologists thought that they stood before an inviolate tomb. In a niche at the end of the shaft, jars and cuts of beef were found, which had certainly been part of a funerary offering. From here, a closed chamber could be reached.

Inside, the treasure of a queen was found who, on the basis of the inscriptions on the grave goods, was identified as Hetepheres, wife of Snefru and mother of Khufu.

The grave goods of Hetepheres, nearly all of which are now displayed in the Egyptian Museum in Cairo, include objects of great value: gold plate, jewels, different types of caskets and containers for make-up, and furniture, which included an armchair and a gilt wood bed of very fine workmanship. To the great astonishment of the archaeologists, the alabaster sarcophagus was empty.

The titulary of Hetepheres, found on the objects of the grave goods, is made up of the most prestigious names for a queen of the Old Kingdom: "Mother of the King, Companion of Horus, Daughter of the God," to which another title must be added, fre-

116 THIS BIRD'S-EYE VIEW SHOWS PART OF THE PAVING IN THE EASTERN TEMPLE OF THE GREAT PYRAMID, TWO OF THE SUBSIDIARY PYRAMIDS AROUND WHICH THE PITS OF THE SACRED BOATS AND THE ENTRANCE TO HETEPHERES' TOMB ARE ARRANGED (G 7000 X).

116-117 THIS BIRD'S-EYE VIEW OF THE GREAT PYRAMID SHOWS THE POSITION OF THE SUBSIDIARY PYRAMIDS AND THE MASTABAS THAT SURROUND KHUFU'S FUNERARY MONUMENT TO THE SOUTH AND THE EAST. THE TOMB OF HETEPHERES WAS FOUND NEXT TO THE SUBSIDIARY PYRAMIDS, IN A PIT WITHOUT SUPERSTRUCTURES (G 7000 X).

quently used in this period, that of Superior of the Female Butchers in the House of Acacia, which recalls the role of the queen as being assimilated with the lioness goddess Sekhmet, in the regeneration of the deceased sovereign. Acacia, the tree sacred to the goddess, indeed represents one of the places of the pharaoh's conception and, after his death, becomes the passage for his rebirth in the afterlife. The rituals of slaughter and offering of the sacrificial animal, celebrated by the goddess herself, were indispensable for the funerary rite – alongside the dances of the priestesses of Sekhmet's harem.

In addition to the queen's body not being present inside the sarcophagus, what was most astonishing was the fact that such a tomb was not covered, like that of the other queens, by an adequate pyramid structure. Reisner contended that the real tomb could be elsewhere and suggested that its location should be sought close to one of the pyramids of Snefru in Dahshur, because queens were usually buried close to their husbands and not near their children. Notwithstanding the other theories expounded, again regarding the plateau of Giza, to date no discovery has been made to explain this issue.

118-119 The photo documents excavation of the tomb of Hetepheres (G 7000 X), mother of Khufu (4th Dynasty), by an American mission in Giza, directed by George Reisner in 1927. In the background we can see a pit with a pulley, and the queen's alabaster sarcophagus being brought to the surface.

118 bottom The images show Queen Hetepheres's bracelet casket, before and after its restoration (Egyptian Museum, Cairo).

119 TOP THE SKETCH MAKES
THE ARRANGEMENT OF QUEEN
HETEPHERES' GRAVE GOODS
EASIER TO UNDERSTAND. WE
CAN SEE THE SARCOPHAGUS,
FURNITURE, NUMEROUS VASES,
A SEDAN-CHAIR, TWO
ARMCHAIRS, AND A SERIES OF
WOODEN PALES.

119 BOTTOM AT THE TIME OF
THE DISCOVERY OF QUEEN
HETEPHERES' BURIAL CHAMBER,
THE FOLLOWING WERE CLEARLY
VISIBLE: AN ALABASTER
SARCOPHAGUS, SEVERAL
WOODEN PALES FOR A SEDAN-

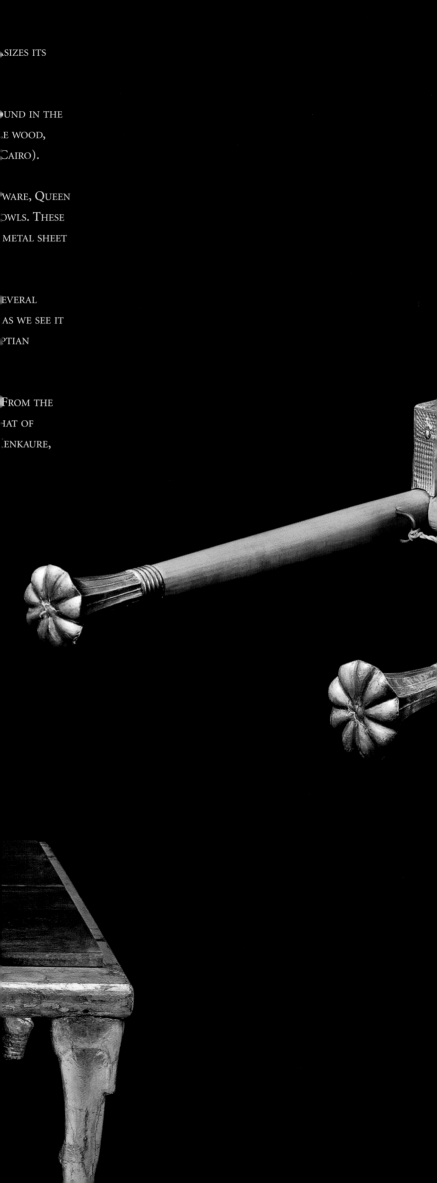

SIZES ITS

UND IN THE
E WOOD,
CAIRO).

WARE, QUEEN
OWLS. THESE
METAL SHEET

EVERAL
AS WE SEE IT
PTIAN

FROM THE
HAT OF
ENKAURE,

The history of another queen is just as problematic. Her name is linked to one of the most interesting literary works of Ancient Egypt. Khentkaus I was the queen and the work is *The Tales of King Khufu*, written on a papyrus known as "The Westcar Papyrus."

The story is rather complicated and is in three parts, which seem to develop independently but on close examination are linked to a very distinct common thread.

The narrative, moving continuously between past, present, and future, introduces the prediction of the birth, after Khufu and his immediate successors, of a dynasty marked by a new concept of sun worship. The mother of its first sovereigns, the literary character Redjedet, wife of a priest of Re, has been identified by some experts as the historical figure of Khentkaus

I, very probably the mother of at least two of the first pharaohs of the 5th Dynasty.

An original funerary monument, which cannot be considered either a conventional *mastaba* or a real pyramid, is dedicated to her, about 500 yards (457 m) southeast of the Pyramid of Khafre. The overall structure is made up of two superimposed architectural elements, built at different times: a square-plan truncated pyramid base dug out of the rock; the walls have a palace façade. It is overlooked by a rectangular-plan building constructed from limestone blocks.

This upper structure was raised on the western side of the base, probably to avoid excessive loading problems on the underground room, and equally probably it was added shortly after the first one. The result is an irregular step pyramid.

124-125 The image hands down to us the traces of the original superstructure of the burial complex of Khentkaus I (late 4th – early 5th Dynasties), comprising a funeral temple, an antechamber, a funeral chamber, and storerooms.

125 left The ambiguous titling of Khentkaus I, etched into a granite portal strut on her tomb, may be interpreted as "Mother of the two Kings of Upper and Lower Egypt," or as "King of Upper and Lower Egypt and Mother of the King of Upper and Lower Egypt."

125 right The image of Khentkaus I etched into the granite portal of her tomb.

A monumental door in pink granite on the eastern side permitted access to the funerary chambers, covered in limestone and decorated with fine relief work. On the external door, the name and titulary of Khentkaus is engraved and this, together with an image of the queen, gave rise to a series of conjectures on the nature of her role.

Indeed, there are two different theories on her titulary, both correct from a grammatical point of view: (1) "Mother of the two Kings of Upper and Lower Egypt"; or (2) "King of Upper and Lower Egypt and Mother of the King of Upper and Lower Egypt." According to the first theory she was the mother of two pharaohs who evidently ruled one after the other; the second suggests that Khentkaus ruled for a certain period (in her own right or as regent of one of her two sons) and that subsequently she was awarded the name Royal Mother.

The special re-fashioning which her image underwent on the granite portal at a second stage would support the latter theory. Indeed, a uraeus was put on her forehead and the false beard on her chin, both signs of regality. As in the case of Merineith, however, the royal name was not in the cartouche. There are further problems regarding the family of Khentkaus: one theory is that the queen was originally the royal wife of Shepseskaf (last sovereign of the 4th Dynasty), and upon his death she married Userkaf (High Priest of Re in Heliopolis and founder of the 5th Dynasty), and from these marriages produced Sahure and Neferirkare, second and third pharaohs respectively of the 5th Dynasty.

There are two more important female figures to remember before the end of the Old Kingdom. The first is the mother of Pepi II, Ankhnesmerire II. One of her most interesting monuments is a small alabaster statue, today in the Brooklyn Museum, which depicts her sitting on the throne with the small pharaoh on her lap. The queen's head is probably decorated with the uraeus, as dictated by the regal role Ankhnesmerire had to fulfill as regent of her son; Pepi II in fact ruled for more than 90 years and became king when he was very young.

The queen, titular of her own pyramid, is furthermore mentioned in numerous documents: one decree mentions her cult together with Queen Neith (one of the wives of Pepi II); one decree for the institution of the cult of one of her statues at Abydos; as well as a rupestrian inscription in the Sinai.

The last sovereign of the 6th Dynasty and first "Pharaoh Queen" of Egyptian history is documented only in a royal list of the Ramesside Period, the so-called "Turin Canon," and from the classical tradition. The Turin Canon refers to Queen Nitocris as King of Upper and Lower Egypt. Her reign could have lasted between two and twelve years but no archaeological document about her has so far come to light. Even though excerpts

from Herodotus and Manetho seem to confirm her existence, her life becomes confused with legend.

Confusion and uncertainty hinder the whole reconstruction of the final phase of the 6th Dynasty: during the long reign of Pepi II, in fact, many of his possible heirs died before him so that succession became extremely problematic.

The end of the 6th Dynasty initiated one of the periods in Egyptian history defined in Egyptology as "intermediate." These were times when the centralized power of the pharaohs dissolved and government was divided among the leading houses. Monumental evidence dwindled to almost nothing, suburban centers and provincial necropolises flourished, but archaeological and textual evidence is insufficient for a thorough historical reconstruction. Indeed, the phase which follows immediately after the end of the Old Kingdom is called the First Intermediate Period and is characterized by a division of the country, in which two ruling houses emerge, after a little-documented period.

The Herakleopolitan princes (of the 9th and 10th dynasties) ruled the north and the Theban princes (11th Dynasty) ruled in the south. One of the last, Mentuhotep Nebhepetre (Mentuhotep II) succeeded in getting the better of his rivals in the north and reunifying Egypt under his rule. The Middle Kingdom was born.

128 THIS CALCITE STATUETTE SHOWS ANKHENESPEPI II (ANKHNESMERIRE II) WITH HER SON PEPI II IN
HER LAP. THE QUEEN'S HEAD IS ADORNED WITH THE VULTURE REMAINS AND HER FOREHEAD HAS A HOLE
WHERE THE URAEUS WOULD HAVE BEEN HOUSED (BROOKLYN MUSEUM, NEW YORK).

129 TOP THE POLYCHROMATIC BAS-RELIEF SHOWS ANKHENESPEPI II ON A BLOCK BROUGHT FROM
SAQQARA. THE PROFILE IS METICULOUSLY CRAFTED AND THE QUEEN'S FACIAL FEATURES ARE SHOWN
WITH GREAT SKILL IN THEIR VARYING DEPTHS. ON HER THERE IS THE SKIN OF A VULTURE, WITH THE
INTACT HEAD PROJECTING OVER THE QUEEN'S FOREHEAD.

129 BOTTOM THE NAME OF ANKHENESPEPI II IS ETCHED ONTO THE SIDE OF THE QUEEN'S SARCOPHAGUS

130-131 This detail of the sarcophagus of Ashayt shows the princess assisted by a handmaiden and a servant, as she holds a lotus flower to her nostrils. Ashayt, whose tomb was found inside the temple of Mentuhotep II at Deir al-Bahari, is defined "King's Mistress and Priestess of Hathor" (Egyptian Museum, Cairo).

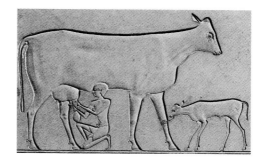

Fine sculptures and tombs with extremely rich tomb furnishings document for the whole period of the Middle Kingdom the existence and importance of a vast number of royal wives.

Inside the grandiose architectural complex alone, built by Mentuhotep II as his own funerary monument at Deir al-Bahari, there are funerary chapels and the relative tombs of six of his wives.

All bear the title Royal Wife and Priestess of Hathor but only one of them, Tem, is defined also as Mother of the King. Elegant painting and fine relief work depict them on the walls of their chapels or on the surfaces of their own sarcophagi. Hair, dress and decoration are very varied: Queen Neferu wears a long wig in three parts and is depicted sitting while a maid styles her hair; Ashayt, also seated, wears a short wig and a white dress which leaves her breast almost visible and she is shown smelling a lotus flower; Kauit wears a short curly wig and is looking at herself in the mirror helped by a servant and a maid: she wears a short cloak over her dress.

131 THE MILKING SCENE ABOVE IS FROM THE SARCOPHAGUS OF KAUIT, A PRINCESS OF THE COURT OF MENTUHOTEP II, AND SHE IS PORTRAYED BELOW AS A HANDMAIDEN COMBS HER HAIR (EGYPTIAN MUSEUM, CAIRO).

132-133 Neferu, one of the royal wives of Mentuhotep II (Nebhepetre) (11th Dynasty), is portrayed on a slab from her rock tomb (TT 319) at Deir al-Bahari, as a handmaiden combs her hair (Brooklyn Museum, New York).

134 TOP THE TWO GOLD BRACELET CLASPS WITH LAPIS LAZULI, TURQUOISE, AND CORNELIAN INLAYS ARE PART OF THE GRAVE GOODS OF KHNUMIT, DAUGHTER OF AMENEMHAT II (EGYPTIAN MUSEUM, CAIRO).

134-135 THE NECKLACE, MADE OF GOLD AND SEMI-PRECIOUS STONES, IS FROM THE GRAVE GOODS OF KHNUMIT (EGYPTIAN MUSEUM, CAIRO).

135 TOP THE GLAZED STEATITE CYLINDER SEAL, FROM AL FAYUM, CONTAINS THE TITLES OF QUEEN SOBEKNEFERU (BRITISH MUSEUM, LONDON).

The most spectacular tombs, however, at least as far as the tomb furnishings are concerned, are those of the queens of the 12th Dynasty: the royal wives were still buried in the small pyramids alongside those of their consorts, and real treasures were found in many of them (in that of Sathathoriunet and al-Lahun, or that of Khnumit in Dahshur, for example). Necklaces, bracelets, earrings, rings, and gold crowns decorated with painted floral motifs or with the regal uraeus, came to light, and often depict natural phenomena, like shells, butterflies, birds, or stars.

Lastly, there is also a pharaoh queen who belonged to the Middle Kingdom: this was Sobekneferu, daughter of Amenemhat III. A statue of her (Louvre E 27135), unfortunately without the head, depicts her with a traditional tight tunic with two

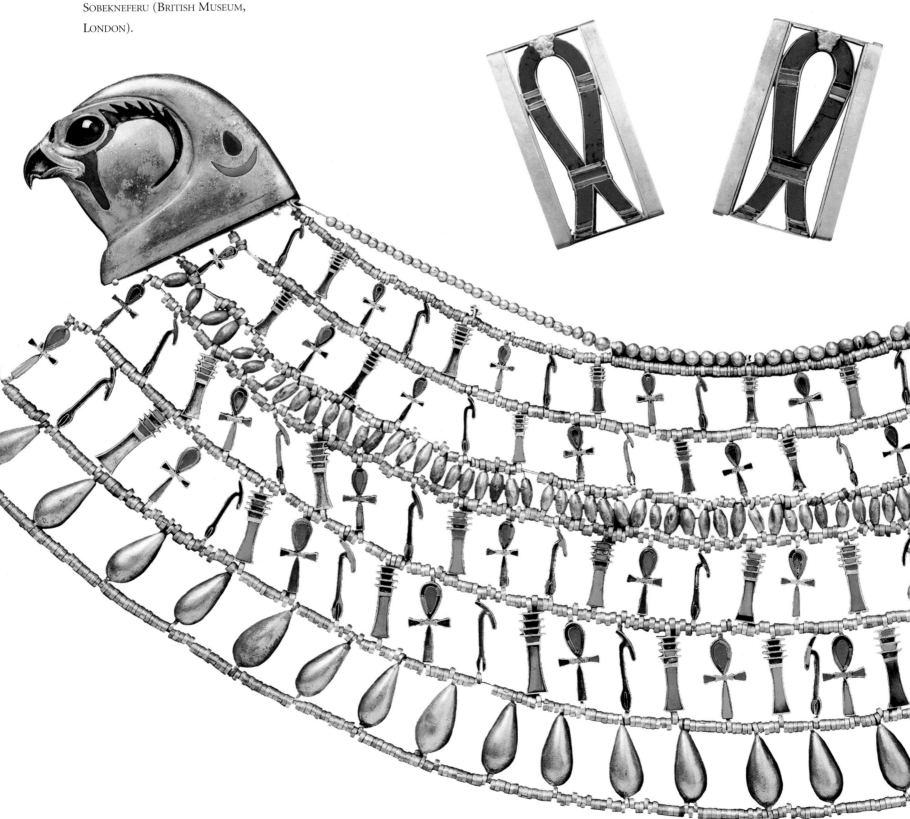

straps, but instead of a wig, the queen was wearing the *nemes*, one of the oldest regal headdresses. The 13th Dynasty and the period immediately after, i.e., the Second Intermediate Period, are characterized by a sequence of reigns which is not always clear. Again a Theban dynasty and a royal house controlling the north of the country battled for power. This time the opponents of the Theban princes were foreign governors, the so-called Hyksos, whose alliances with peoples outside Egypt are well-known, above all with the Nubian kingdoms. From the time of Tao II, one of the last princes of the 17th Dynasty, the Thebans began the battle for reunification of the country, which marked the beginning of one of the most splendid periods in Egyptian history: the New Kingdom.

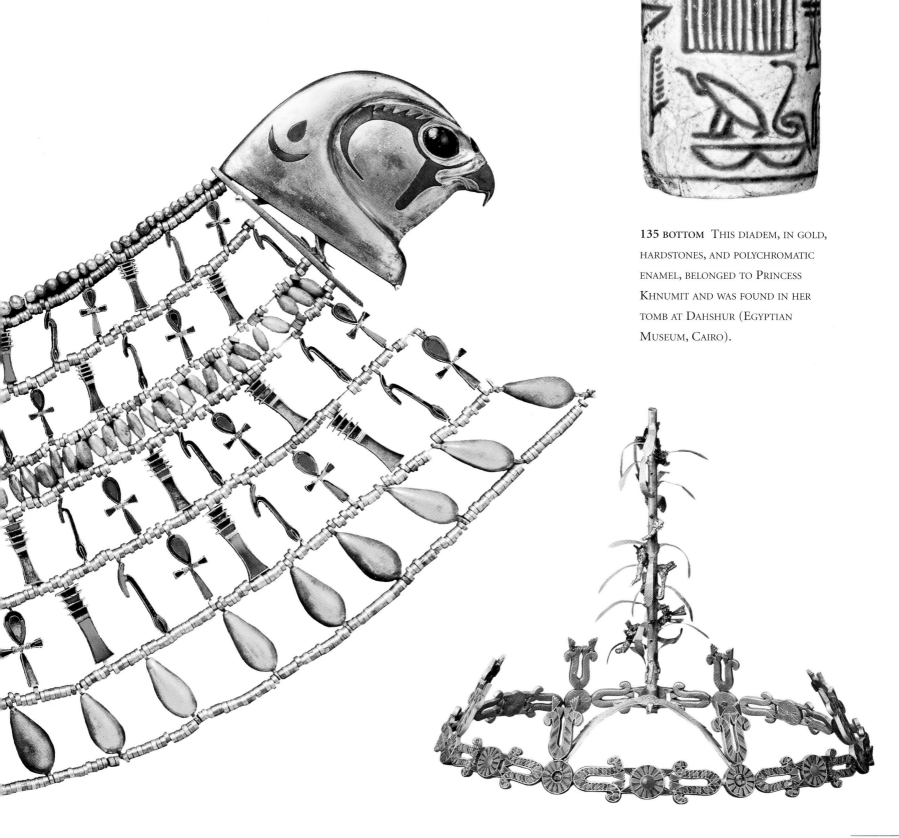

135 BOTTOM THIS DIADEM, IN GOLD, HARDSTONES, AND POLYCHROMATIC ENAMEL, BELONGED TO PRINCESS KHNUMIT AND WAS FOUND IN HER TOMB AT DAHSHUR (EGYPTIAN MUSEUM, CAIRO).

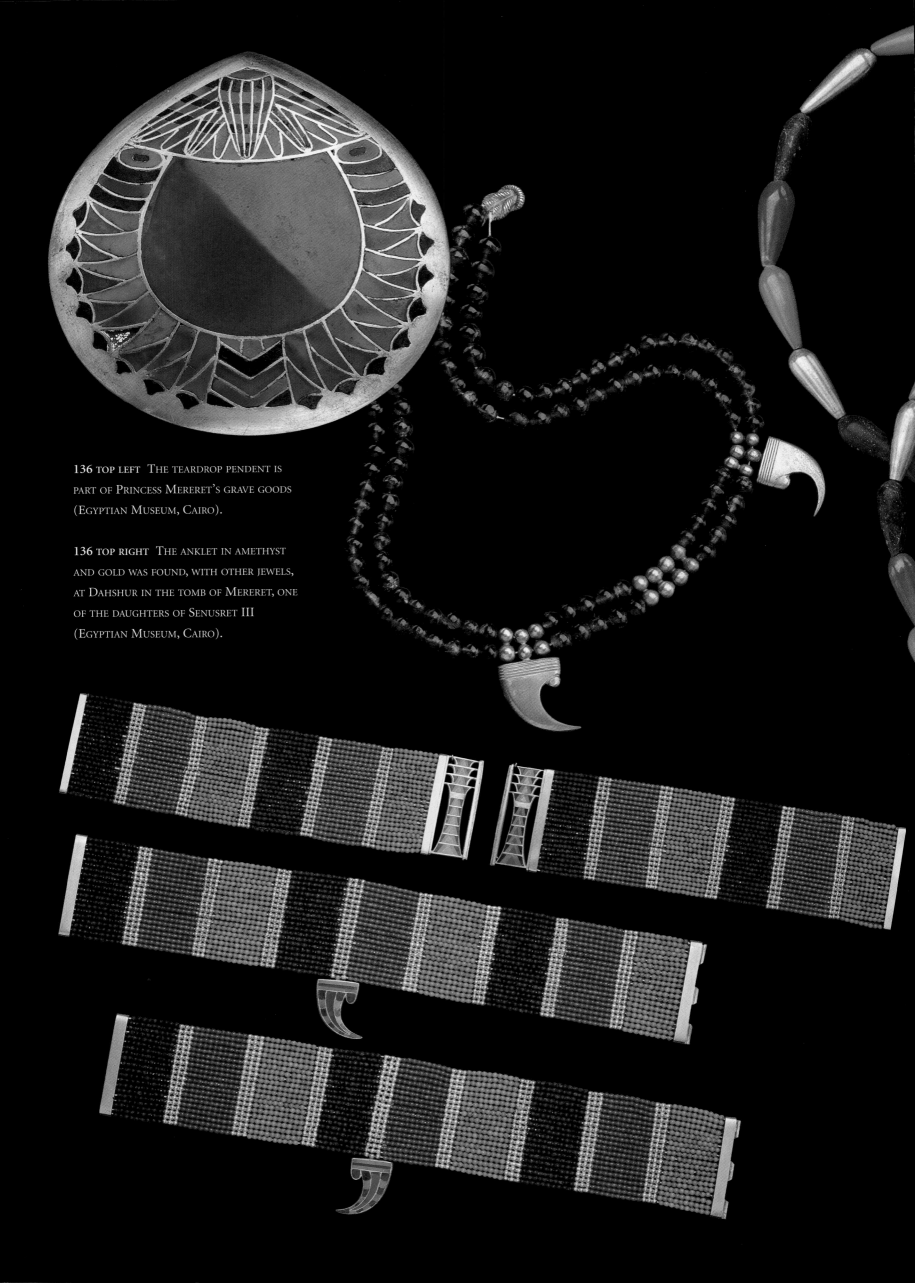

136 TOP LEFT THE TEARDROP PENDENT IS
PART OF PRINCESS MERERET'S GRAVE GOODS
(EGYPTIAN MUSEUM, CAIRO).

136 TOP RIGHT THE ANKLET IN AMETHYST
AND GOLD WAS FOUND, WITH OTHER JEWELS,
AT DAHSHUR IN THE TOMB OF MERERET, ONE
OF THE DAUGHTERS OF SENUSRET III
(EGYPTIAN MUSEUM, CAIRO).

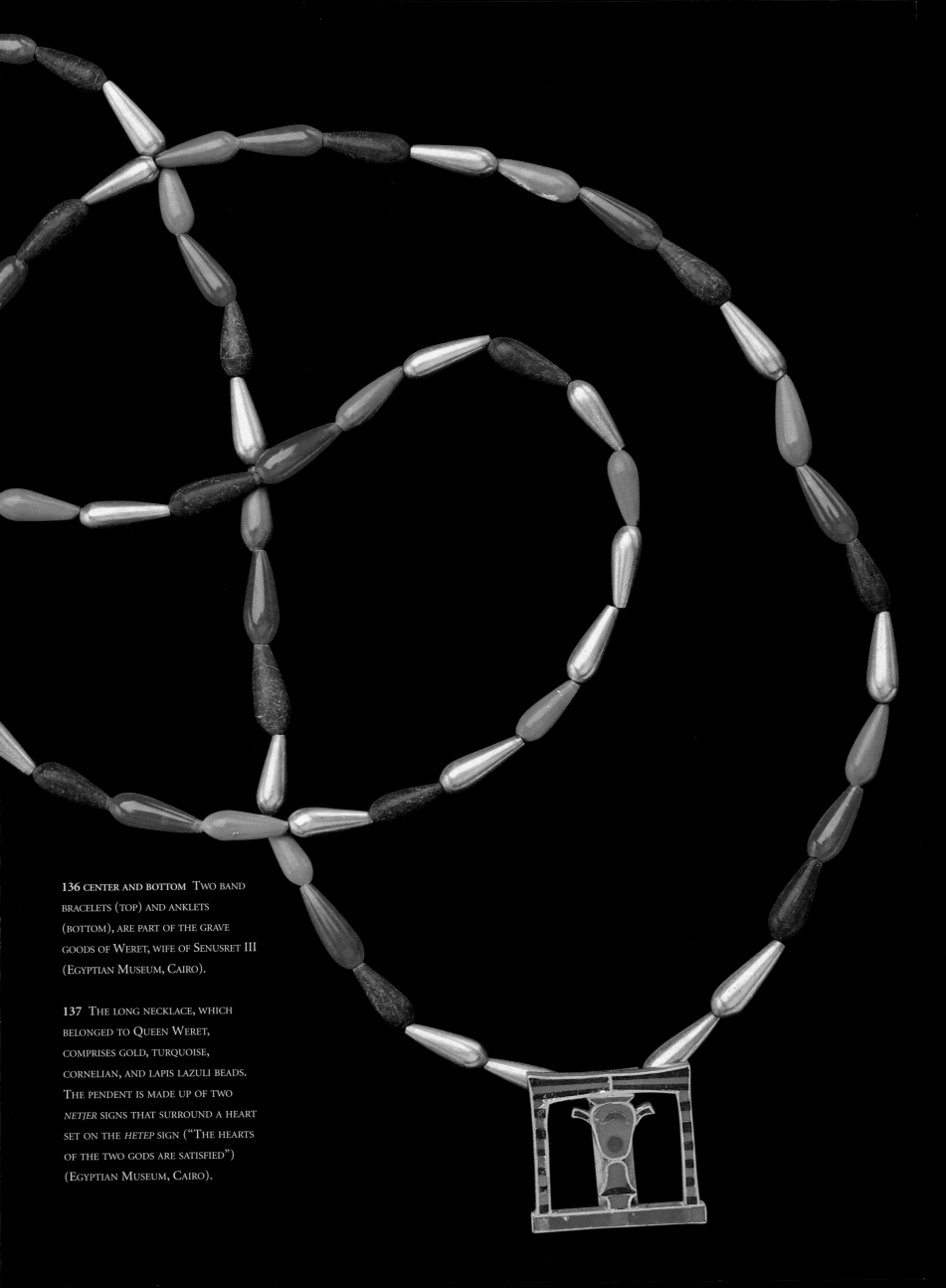

136 CENTER AND BOTTOM TWO BAND
BRACELETS (TOP) AND ANKLETS
(BOTTOM), ARE PART OF THE GRAVE
GOODS OF WERET, WIFE OF SENUSRET III
(EGYPTIAN MUSEUM, CAIRO).

137 THE LONG NECKLACE, WHICH
BELONGED TO QUEEN WERET,
COMPRISES GOLD, TURQUOISE,
CORNELIAN, AND LAPIS LAZULI BEADS.
THE PENDENT IS MADE UP OF TWO
NETJER SIGNS THAT SURROUND A HEART
SET ON THE *HETEP* SIGN ("THE HEARTS
OF THE TWO GODS ARE SATISFIED")
(EGYPTIAN MUSEUM, CAIRO).

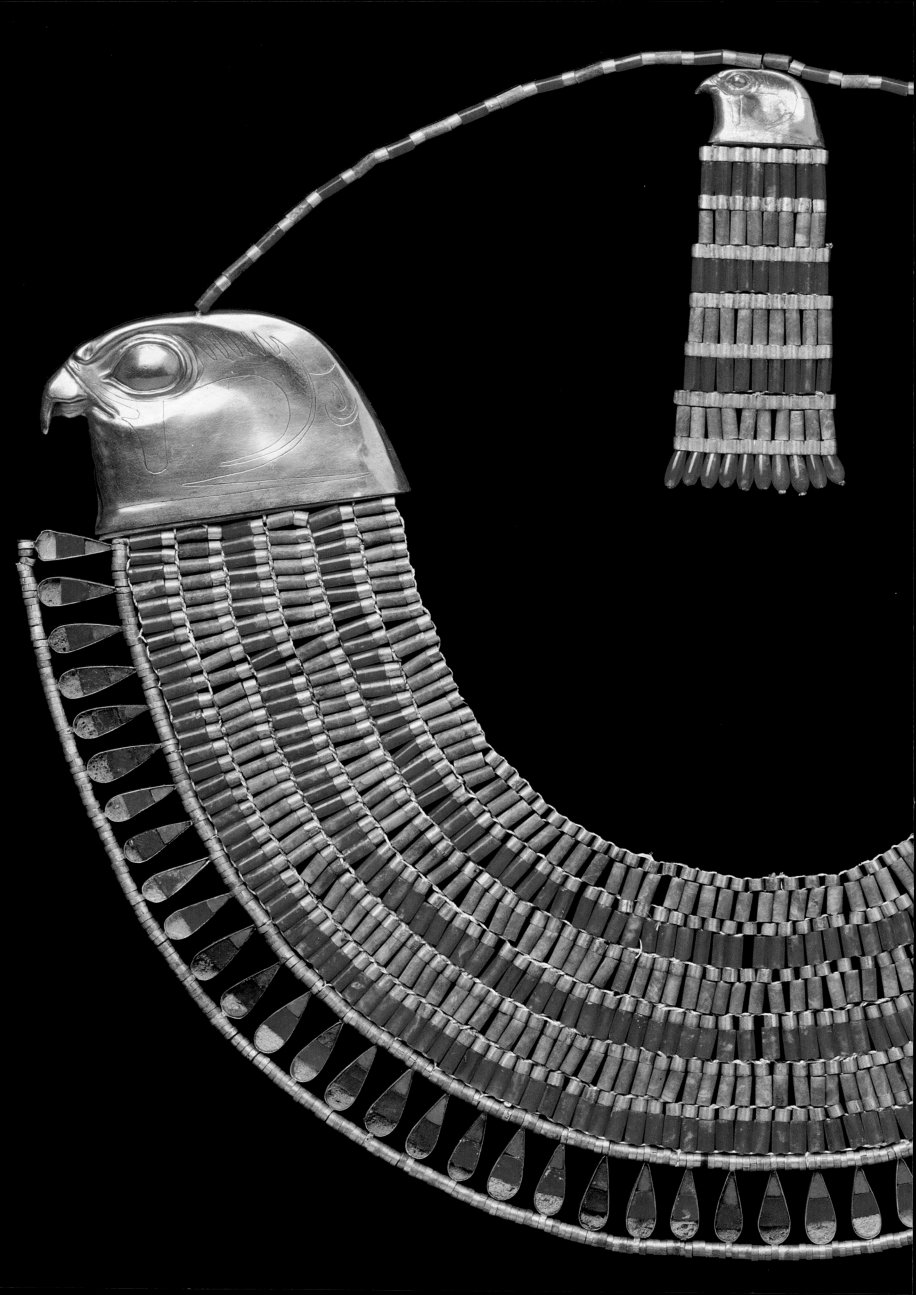

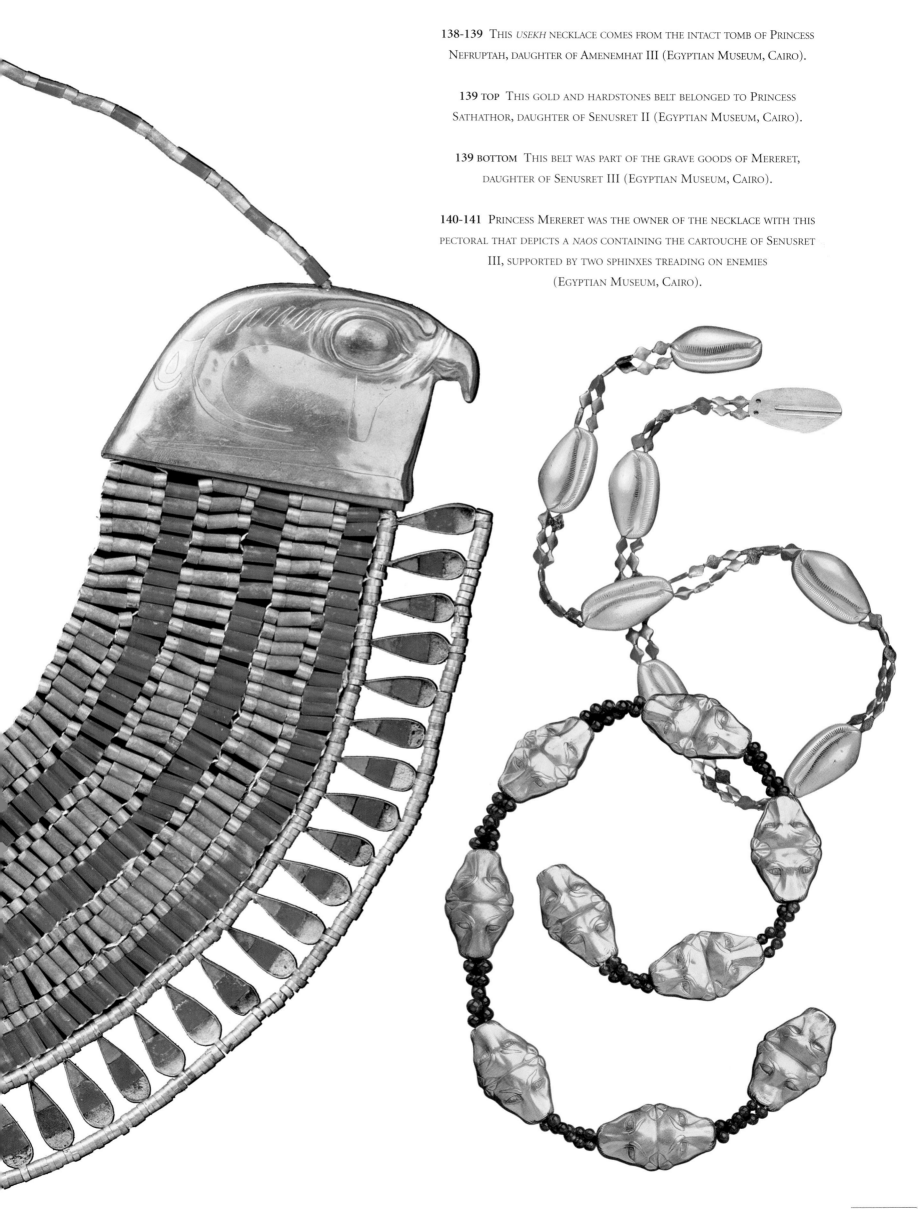

138-139 This *usekh* necklace comes from the intact tomb of Princess Nefruptah, daughter of Amenemhat III (Egyptian Museum, Cairo).

139 top This gold and hardstones belt belonged to Princess Sathathor, daughter of Senusret II (Egyptian Museum, Cairo).

139 bottom This belt was part of the grave goods of Mereret, daughter of Senusret III (Egyptian Museum, Cairo).

140-141 Princess Mereret was the owner of the necklace with this pectoral that depicts a *naos* containing the cartouche of Senusret III, supported by two sphinxes treading on enemies (Egyptian Museum, Cairo).

THE NEW KINGDOM

142 THE GILT WOOD SARCOPHAGUS BELONGS TO THE GREAT ROYAL WIFE AHHOTEP I, A HIGHLY PRESTIGIOUS FIGURE OF THE 17TH AND 18TH DYNASTIES (EGYPTIAN MUSEUM, CAIRO).

143 THE IMAGE SHOWS THE ARCH OF THE STELE THAT AHMOSE, FIRST SOVEREIGN OF THE 18TH DYNASTY, ERECTED AT ABYDOS, IN HONOR OF HIS GRANDMOTHER TETISHERI (EGYPTIAN MUSEUM, CAIRO).

It appears evident from the documentation of the 18th Dynasty that the role of the queens was of vital importance, both in the war to vanquish the Hyksos and in ruling the newly pacified country. Indeed, in their titularies, descriptions such as Lady of the Two Lands or Lady of Upper and Lower Egypt appear constantly at this time. It was the sovereigns themselves who dedicated great respect and devotion to their ancestors or their wives, and erected monuments to them to recall their achievements.

Ahmose, the first sovereign of the 18th Dynasty, dedicated two interesting monuments to the women of the royal family: he erected a cenotaph in Abydos, to his grandmother, Queen Tetisheri, the remains of which look very much like a pyramid; and he dedicated a stele in the temple of Karnak to his mother, Queen Ahhotep I. We learn from this second document that Ahhotep's intervention during some of the phases of the battle against the Hyksos was decisive.

The sovereign indeed urged: "Give your praise to the Lady of the Lands of the North, whose name is exalted in all foreign countries, to she who rules the multitudes, who looks after Egypt with wisdom, who took care of its army, who watched over the country and made the fugitives return and reunited the deserters, who appeased Egypt and subdued the rebels."

It is evident from these words that, at a certain point of Ahmose's reign, Ahhotep acted as sovereign, exercising a regal role, very probably as regent for her son. Further documents confirm her role as a "fighting pharaoh."

In a tomb at Dra Abu al-Naga, discovered by the pioneer French Egyptologist Auguste Mariette in 1850, precious tomb furnishings were brought to light, associated with a female mummy, whose name was Ahhotep. Because the queen's sarcophagus was in fact found later in another tomb (TT 320, the so-called *cache* of Deir al-Bahari, where during the 21st Dynasty the mummies of many pharaohs and queens of the New Kingdom whose tombs had been violated and plundered were moved) some experts have suggested that the body in the tomb at Dra Abu al-Naga is not that of Ahhotep I, mother of Ahmose, but somebody else of the same name, wife of Kamose, last sovereign of the 18th Dynasty, and predecessor of Ahmose.

The tomb furnishings, however, seem to be entirely appropriate for the image of the queen handed down to us from the stele of Karnak. As well as very fine jewels, other objects found included: a gold dagger; a hatchet with a wooden handle covered in gold, on which there is the characteristic scene of the sovereign as sphinx trampling the enemy; and a gold necklace with large fly-shaped pendants, usually awarded for military valor.

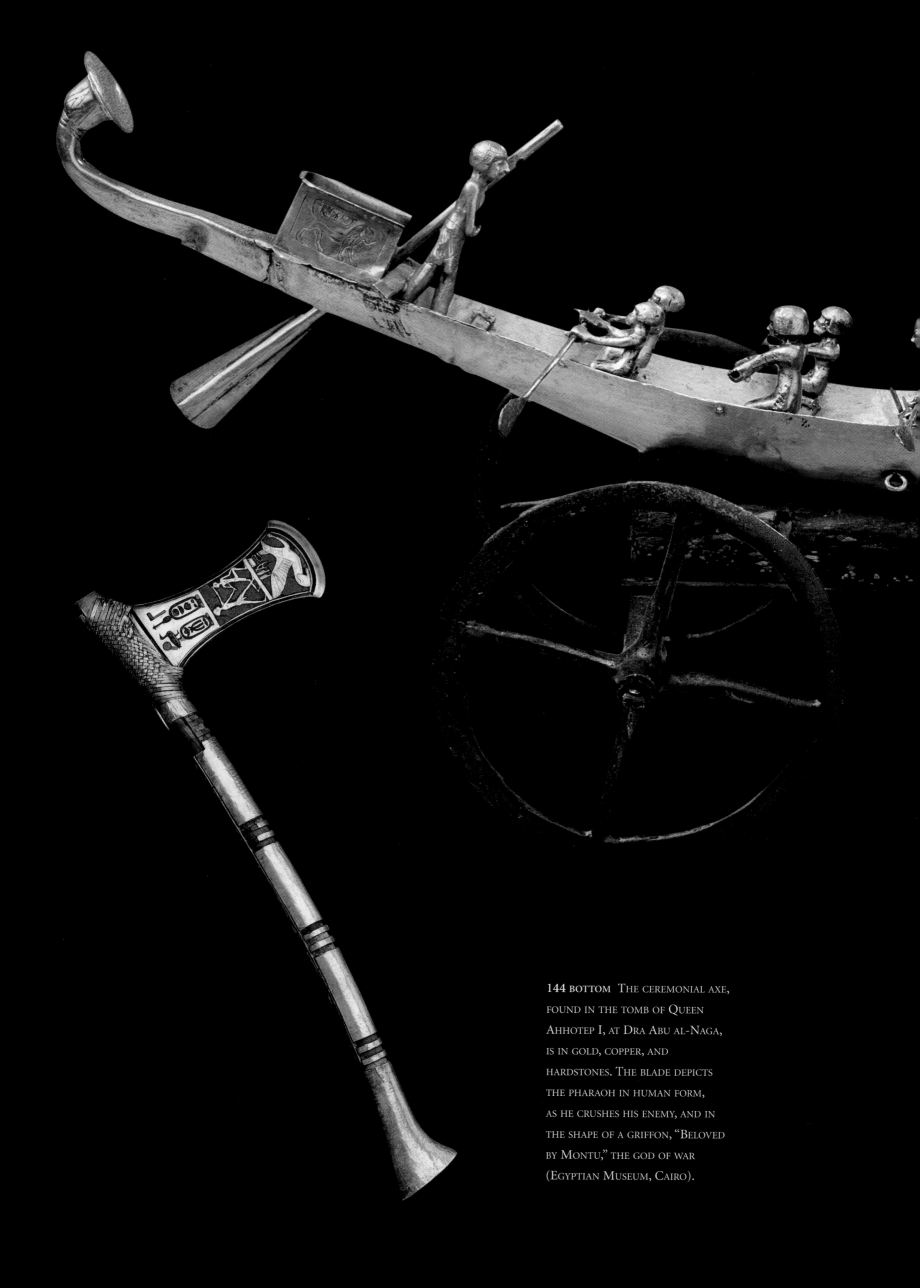

144 bottom The ceremonial axe, found in the tomb of Queen Ahhotep I, at Dra Abu al-Naga, is in gold, copper, and hardstones. The blade depicts the pharaoh in human form, as he crushes his enemy, and in the shape of a griffon, "Beloved by Montu," the god of war (Egyptian Museum, Cairo).

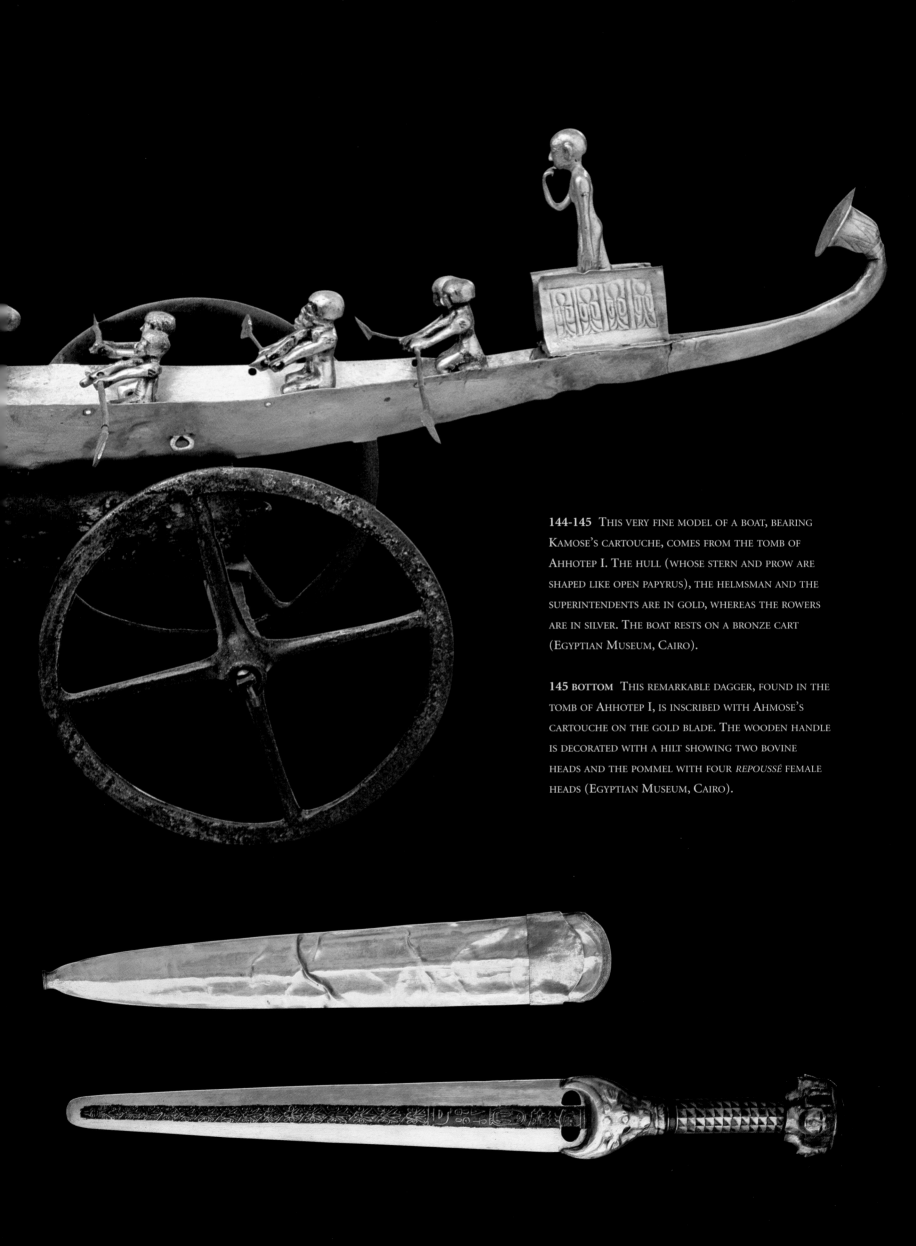

144-145 THIS VERY FINE MODEL OF A BOAT, BEARING KAMOSE'S CARTOUCHE, COMES FROM THE TOMB OF AHHOTEP I. THE HULL (WHOSE STERN AND PROW ARE SHAPED LIKE OPEN PAPYRUS), THE HELMSMAN AND THE SUPERINTENDENTS ARE IN GOLD, WHEREAS THE ROWERS ARE IN SILVER. THE BOAT RESTS ON A BRONZE CART (EGYPTIAN MUSEUM, CAIRO).

145 BOTTOM THIS REMARKABLE DAGGER, FOUND IN THE TOMB OF AHHOTEP I, IS INSCRIBED WITH AHMOSE'S CARTOUCHE ON THE GOLD BLADE. THE WOODEN HANDLE IS DECORATED WITH A HILT SHOWING TWO BOVINE HEADS AND THE POMMEL WITH FOUR *REPOUSSÉ* FEMALE HEADS (EGYPTIAN MUSEUM, CAIRO).

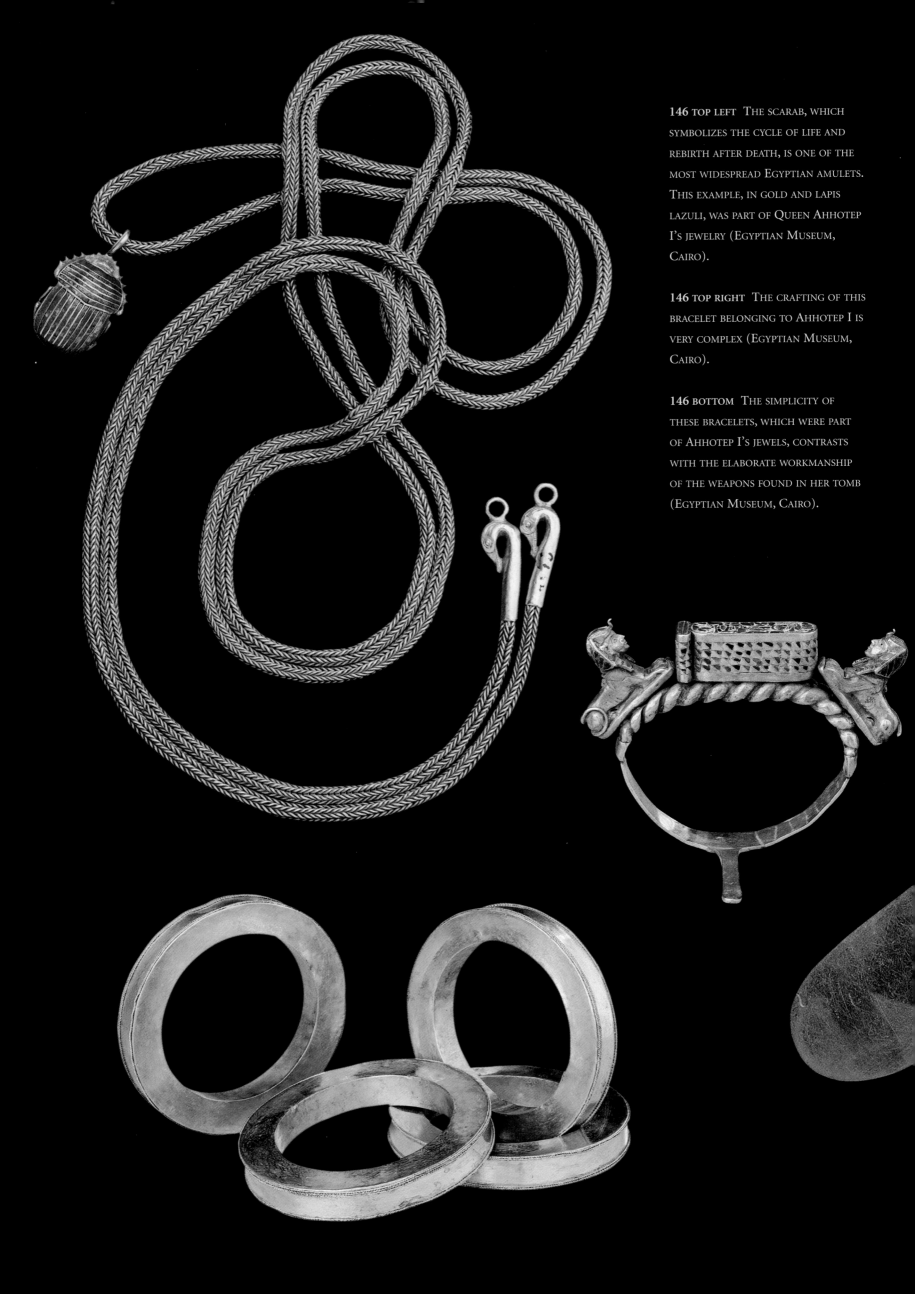

146 TOP LEFT THE SCARAB, WHICH
SYMBOLIZES THE CYCLE OF LIFE AND
REBIRTH AFTER DEATH, IS ONE OF THE
MOST WIDESPREAD EGYPTIAN AMULETS.
THIS EXAMPLE, IN GOLD AND LAPIS
LAZULI, WAS PART OF QUEEN AHHOTEP
I'S JEWELRY (EGYPTIAN MUSEUM,
CAIRO).

146 TOP RIGHT THE CRAFTING OF THIS
BRACELET BELONGING TO AHHOTEP I IS
VERY COMPLEX (EGYPTIAN MUSEUM,
CAIRO).

146 BOTTOM THE SIMPLICITY OF
THESE BRACELETS, WHICH WERE PART
OF AHHOTEP I'S JEWELS, CONTRASTS
WITH THE ELABORATE WORKMANSHIP
OF THE WEAPONS FOUND IN HER TOMB
(EGYPTIAN MUSEUM, CAIRO).

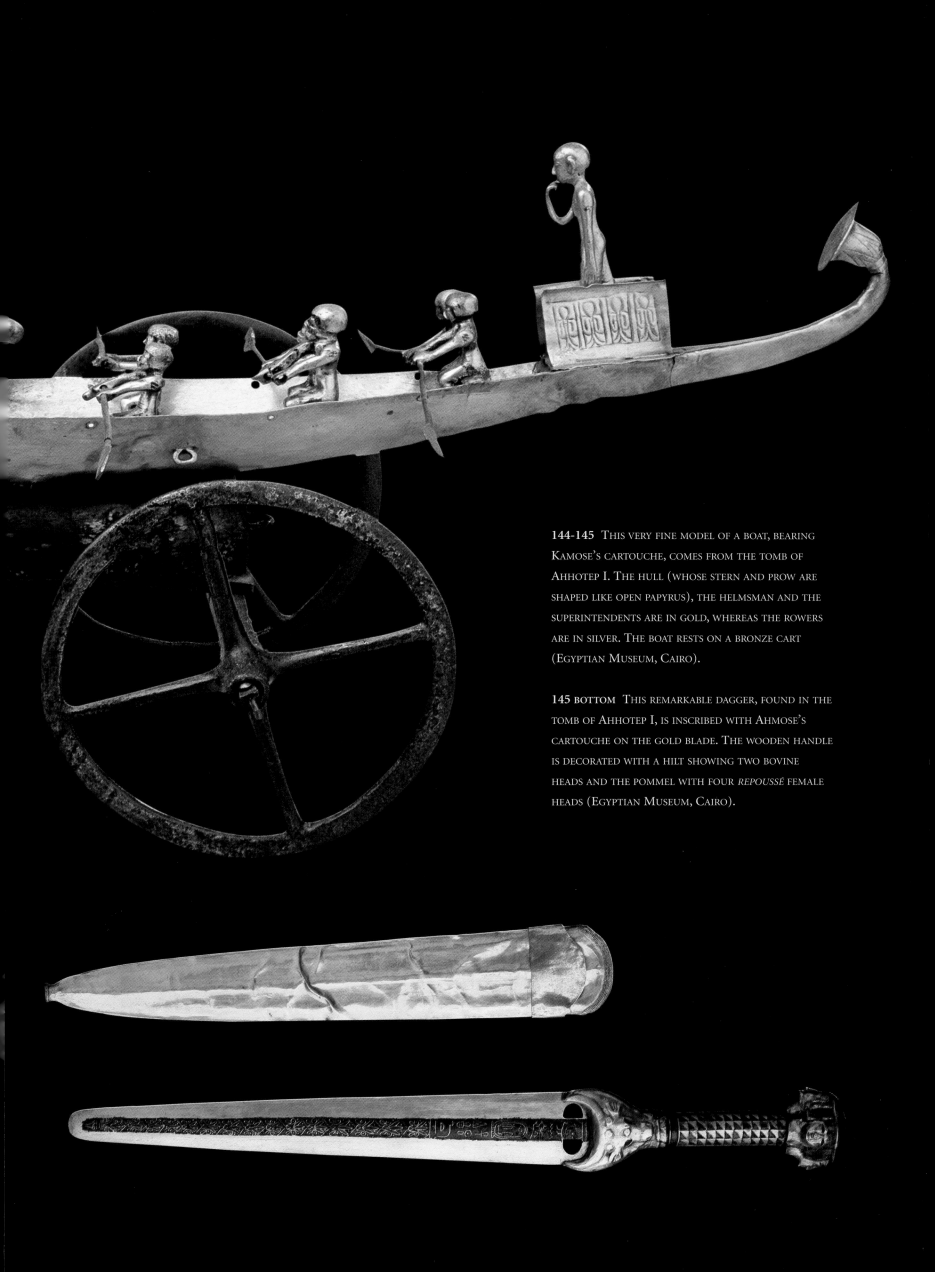

144-145 This very fine model of a boat, bearing Kamose's cartouche, comes from the tomb of Ahhotep I. The hull (whose stern and prow are shaped like open papyrus), the helmsman and the superintendents are in gold, whereas the rowers are in silver. The boat rests on a bronze cart (Egyptian Museum, Cairo).

145 bottom This remarkable dagger, found in the tomb of Ahhotep I, is inscribed with Ahmose's cartouche on the gold blade. The wooden handle is decorated with a hilt showing two bovine heads and the pommel with four *repoussé* female heads (Egyptian Museum, Cairo).

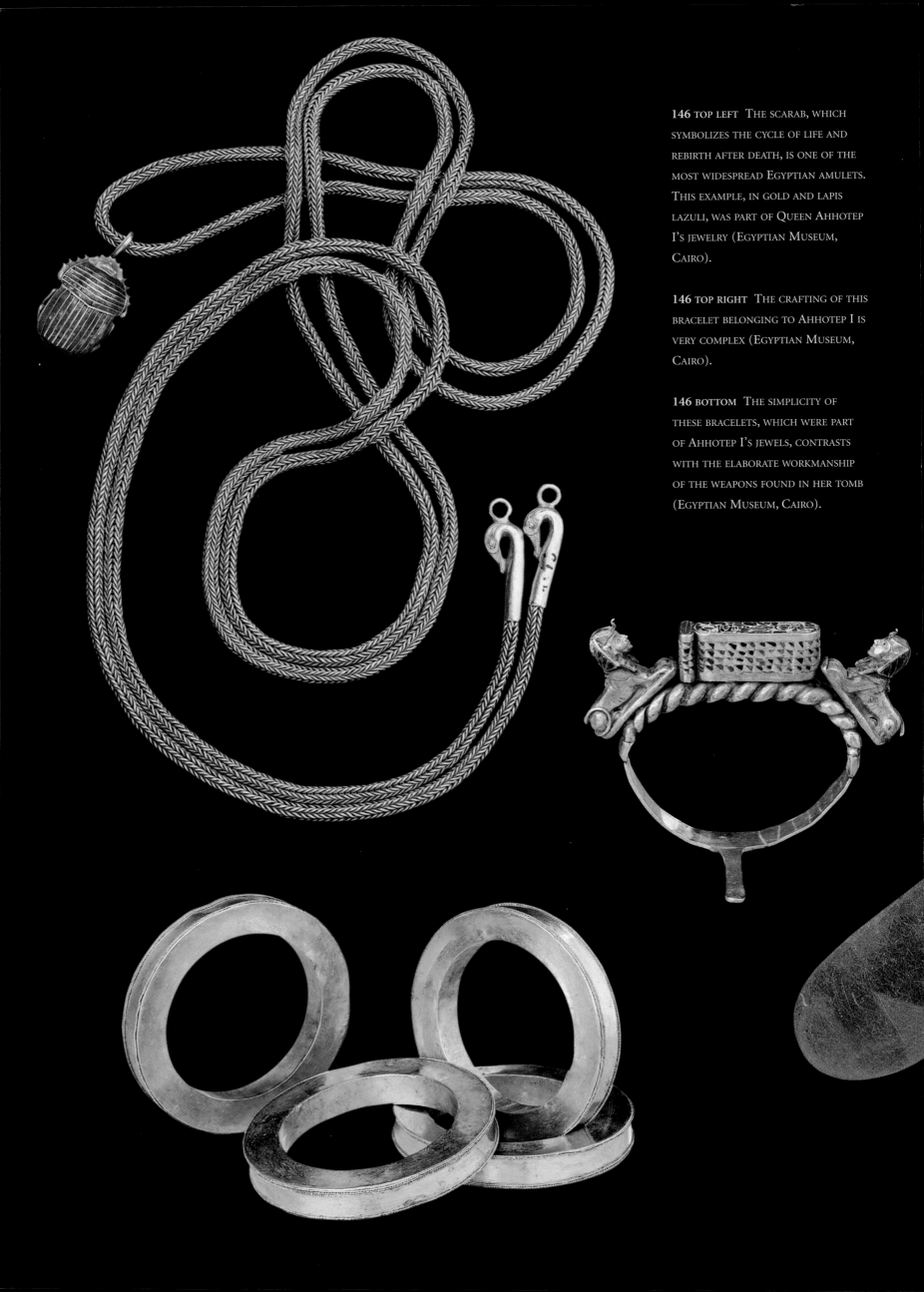

146 top left The scarab, which symbolizes the cycle of life and rebirth after death, is one of the most widespread Egyptian amulets. This example, in gold and lapis lazuli, was part of Queen Ahhotep I's jewelry (Egyptian Museum, Cairo).

146 top right The crafting of this bracelet belonging to Ahhotep I is very complex (Egyptian Museum, Cairo).

146 bottom The simplicity of these bracelets, which were part of Ahhotep I's jewels, contrasts with the elaborate workmanship of the weapons found in her tomb (Egyptian Museum, Cairo).

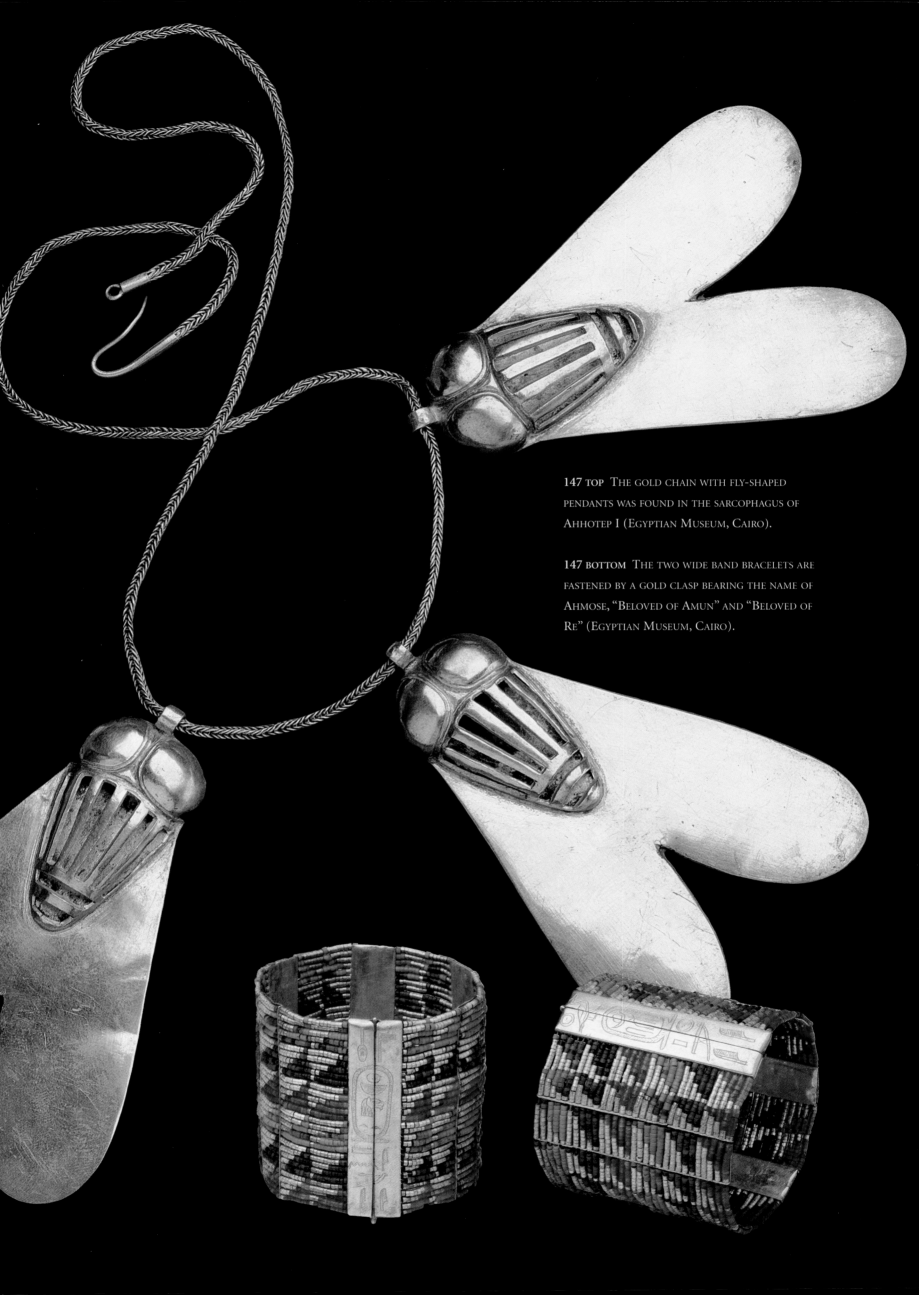

147 TOP THE GOLD CHAIN WITH FLY-SHAPED PENDANTS WAS FOUND IN THE SARCOPHAGUS OF AHHOTEP I (EGYPTIAN MUSEUM, CAIRO).

147 BOTTOM THE TWO WIDE BAND BRACELETS ARE FASTENED BY A GOLD CLASP BEARING THE NAME OF AHMOSE, "BELOVED OF AMUN" AND "BELOVED OF RE" (EGYPTIAN MUSEUM, CAIRO).

But the reign of Ahmose is characterized by another significant female presence. Like his father before him, the sovereign had married his own sister, Ahmes-Nefertari, who had assumed the role of Great Royal Wife and who subsequently also became Mother of the King. The figure of Ahmes-Nefertari is nonetheless to be remembered for another important event, i.e., the institution of a religious foundation with female clergy, dedicated to the cult of the god Amun, whose priestesses were called God's Wives of Amun.

We have already had the possibility of introducing and mentioning the repercussions that this foundation could have had upon the determination of royal succession. The text of a stele, found in the temple of Karnak, briefly describes the foundation and the principal economic effects. Ahmes-Nerfertari renounced the title of Second Priest of Amun in exchange for the means to create an economic and religious foundation, like the God's Wives of Amun, whose fortune comprised furniture and property of considerable proportions like a dwelling, lands, jewels, ointments, and clothes.

The text of the stele explains that "the queen became rich, when she was poor" and that these goods "must pass from son to son, for eternity," according to a well-known formula of Egyptian law. There is no doubt that the political, economic, and religious value of this institution must have been considerable: suffice it to say that the queen became, to all intents and purposes, the female counterpart of the High Priest of Amun, the most important exponent of the Theban clergy.

The power and prestige she must have enjoyed, both in political and religious fields, is confirmed by the fact that one of the first Houses of Millions of Years, built by the sovereigns on the west bank of the Thebes, was attributed to Ahmes-Nefertari (and to her son Amenhotep I). Indeed, her long life (she died during the reign of her son's successor) was characterized by assiduous rule: her strong presence is documented both during the reign of her husband Ahmose and during that of Amenhotep I, for whom she also acted as regent; her influence did not even diminish in later stages of Amenhotep I's reign, partly because the king was quickly widowed and there is no evidence of any other spouse after the first wife.

Upon her death, Ahmes-Nefertari was deified together with her son, with whom she became Patron of the Theban Necropolis. Their image is present in numerous tombs of prominent people of the capital and numerous *ex-voto* offerings, such as scarabs, statues, stelae, and sistra bearing her name were dedicated, in particular, to the queen. Her mummy, which lay in a monumental sarcophagus in the tomb of Dra Abu al-Naga, was subsequently moved to the *cache* of Deir al-Bahari and is now in the Egyptian Museum in Cairo.

148 AND 149 THE WOODEN STATUETTE, FROM THE VILLAGE OF DEIR AL-MEDINA, SHOWS THE DEIFIED QUEEN AHMES-NEFERTARI AND DATES BACK TO THE REIGN OF RAMESSES II. THE SOVEREIGN, SHOWN IN WALKING POSE ON A PARALLELEPIPED BASE, WEARS A CLOSE-FITTING PLEATED TUNIC AND HOLDS A FAN IN HER LEFT HAND (THE LOUVRE, PARIS).

150 This stele of the Ramesside period comes from Deir al-Medina and is dedicated to Amenhotep I and his mother Ahmes-Nefertari, shown in the upper order opposite Osiris and Anubis. The lower orders show the usual scenes of funeral offerings (The Louvre, Paris).

151 The stele, from Deir al-Medina, represents one of the many *ex-voto* dedicated to Pharaoh Amenhotep I and his mother Ahmes-Nefertari, deified and worshipped during the Ramesside period. The lower order portrays the offerors on their knees with their arms lifted in the sign of prayer (Egyptian Museum, Turin).

We need not go much further forward in the history of the 18th Dynasty to find another important female figure: Hatshepsut is without doubt one of the Egyptian queens who has aroused most interest in both researchers and Egyptologists.

Hatshepsut was the daughter of Thutmosis I, God's Wife of Amun and Great Royal Wife of Thutmosis II. She effectively began to rule Egypt after the premature (?) death of her husband and step-brother. The royal couple had had only one daughter, Neferure, while the only possible male heir, Thutmosis III, born to a second wife, Aset, must have been only four or five years old at the time. A document found in the tomb of Ieni, one of the functionaries of the time, describes the succession to the throne of Thutmosis II as follows: "Thutmosis rose toward the sky and joined the gods. His son took his place as King of Upper and Lower Egypt and reigned on the throne of he who had created him. His sister, the God's Wife, Hatshepsut, ruled the country. The two lands submitted to her will and served her . . . ." Once again a queen ruled while awaiting the heir's coming of age. In this case, however, it was not her son and according to the interpretation suggested in the first chapter of this book, he was not a prince who had been destined to rule, unless he was joined in matrimony with a God's Wife. Notwithstanding this, the first seven years of the reign seem to have passed according to the rules of normal regency, which should have ended when Thutmosis III came of age.

Hatshepsut ruled the country, sent trade expeditions, and is depicted carrying out regal ceremonies, while maintaining her title as queen and royal wife. She nonetheless undertook a series of activities little suited to a temporary sovereign: it would appear that both the project for the erection of her first obelisks in the Temple of Karnak and the preparation of projects for the construction of her House of Millions of Years on the west bank of Thebes, belong to this period.

An important change occurred during the seventh year of the reign; given the documentation available to us, it seems to probably have occurred concurrently with the expiry of the regency period. It appears evident that it was Hatshepsut who succeeded to the throne as King of Upper and Lower Egypt, while Thutmosis III began to be shown as a co-regent, and always in a secondary role, behind the queen. Despite this, the years of the reign are counted from the succession to the throne of Thutmosis III and refer to both the sovereigns.

Upon her coronation, Hatshepsut handed on her role as God's Wife to her daughter Neferure and assumed not only regal apparel but even acquired a masculine appearance: her new iconography included the regal *shendyt* kilt, leaving the torso bare, the *nemes*, and the false beard, while her titulary comprised five canonic names: the name of Horus "Powerful of Ka," the Two Ladies "Flourishing in Years," Golden Horus "Divine of Apparitions," King of Upper and Lower Egypt "Maatkare," and Daughter of Re "She who joins Amun, Hatshepsut."

152 The *pyramidion* of the fallen obelisk of Karnak is etched with the scene of Amun-Re laying his hands on the head of Hatshepsut: the queen kneels before the god, who concedes "the regality of the two lands." This is the final phase of the coronation ceremony.

153 The image shows a block of the so-called Red Chapel that Hatshepsut ordered to be built in the Karnak Temple.

154-155 This particular type of sphinx, in painted limestone, shows Hatshepsut with a human face and a lion's mane. Under the fake beard there is the cartouche with the queen's coronation name of "Maatkare" (Egyptian Museum, Cairo).

155 Hatshepsut, with a snood and a *uraeus* on her forehead, is portrayed kneeling as she offers a vase supported by a *djed* column. The pink granite sculpture must have been part of the sculptural furnishings of the temple of Deir al-Bahari, probably set into one of the niches in the third courtyard (Egyptian Museum, Berlin).

156-157 THIS PINK GRANITE PORTRAIT OF HATSHEPSUT RESEMBLES THE PORTRAITURE OF THUTMOSIS III. ALTHOUGH THE MOUTH IS DELICATE AND SMILING SLIGHTLY, THE SIZE AND PROPORTIONS OF THE NOSE AND EYES RECALL SEVERAL PORTRAITS OF THE QUEEN'S SUCCESSOR (EGYPTIAN MUSEUM, BERLIN).

157 THE SCULPTURE SHOWS A RARE IMAGE OF PHARAOH HATSHEPSUT IN REGAL GARB BUT WITH FEMALE FEATURES. THE LIMESTONE SCULPTURE IS SLIGHTLY BIGGER THAN LIFE-SIZE BUT IS OF HARMONIOUS PROPORTIONS, EXPRESSING AT THE SAME TIME STRENGTH AND SERENITY (METROPOLITAN MUSEUM OF ART, NEW YORK).

Probably in the course of the following year, the construction of the House of Millions of Years was begun in Deir al-Bahari. Construction continued throughout the reign but was never completed and the temple, which in Ancient Egyptian was called *Djeser Djeseru* ("The Sublime of Sublimes") fitted in perfectly with the splendid scenery of the Qurna hills, immediately to the north of the funerary temple which Mentuhotep II Nebhepetre had had built for himself almost 600 years before.

Hatshepsut wanted to pay homage to her illustrious ancestor, the re-unifier of Egypt after the First Intermediate Period, not only building her own temple in its immediate vicinity but also

recapturing, in part, its architecture. The *Djeser Djeseru* is built in three sloping tiers, bounded by arcades with colonnades and pillars, ending with a double sanctuary, hewn out of the rock, dedicated to Amun-Re. The arcades of the middle tier are flanked by two chapels dedicated to the goddess Hathor and the god Anubis (to the south and north respectively), the third tier, to the south, on the other hand, houses two chapels of a funerary type (one for the queen, the other for her father) and to the north, an uncovered courtyard has a sun altar.

The whole temple was decorated with sculptures representing the queen: avenues lined with sphinxes flanked the ramp of

the temple up to the entrance and along the two terraces; Osirid pillars of the queen dominated from the arcade of the third tier, while peristyle niches permitted access to the sanctuary of the boat of the god Amun, they contained standing and kneeling sculptures of the queen making offerings to the gods. A statue of the god and his boat were placed – during feasts – in the two sanctuaries carved out of the rock.

On the walls of the arcades and the chapels, texts and portraits, with very fine relief work and which were made according to themes we can divide into four main sections: (1) portrayals of important feats and annual ceremonies which took place at Deir al-Bahari and in other Theban temples; (2) scenes of offering and adoration dedicated to the god Amun and other "guest" deities, especially Hathor and Anubis; (3) portrayals and texts which had the objective of depicting the divine nature of the queen/pharaoh; and (4) portrayals and texts celebrating the principal events which had characterized her reign and which were dedicated to the Theban god.

For the first time, an Egyptian sovereign presented his own image through the figurative and textual program of one of his monuments, explained the thoughts underlying his achievements and permitting us to reconstruct, almost year by year, the events which, according to his thought deserved to be selected to represent his own reign. These are the main events:

(1) the transportation of two large obelisks from Aswan to be placed at the eastern entrance of the temple of Karnak, where Hatshepsut had erected the first nucleus of a new sanctuary;

(2) the magnificent commercial expedition to Punt, an exotic land from which the Egyptians obtained numerous luxury products, among which was *antiu* – a prized incense. *Antiu* was indispensable for divine ceremonies because the deity manifested himself through its perfume;

(3) the conception of the queen by the god Amun, who, taking on human appearance, joins the wife of the reigning sovereign;

(4) Hatshepsut's pilgrimage with her father to visit the temples of the south and north; and

(5) the complex ceremonies linked to the coronation of the queen at the wish of the god Amun himself.

158-159 THIS AERIAL VIEW SHOWS THE HEMICYCLE OF DEIR AL-BAHARI (WEST THEBES), INCLUDING THE TEMPLE OF MENTUHOTEP NEBHEPETRE, LEFT (11TH DYNASTY), AND THE TEMPLE OF HATSHEPSUT, RIGHT (18TH DYNASTY); THE SANCTUARY OF THUTMOSIS III IS BETWEEN THE TWO.

160-161 THE OSIRIAN COLOSSI OF HATSHEPSUT DECORATE THE COLUMNS OF THE THIRD TERRACE AT THE TEMPLE OF DEIR AL-BAHARI, AND LEAD INTO THE MORE INTIMATE AREA COMPRISED OF THE "FEAST COURT" AND THE SANCTUARIES DEDICATED TO AMUN, THE WORSHIP OF OSIRIS, AND OF THE SUN.

162 SEVERAL BLOCKS OF THE PUNT PORTICO HAVE BEEN REMOVED FROM
THEIR ORIGINAL LOCATION AND ARE NOW IN THE EGYPTIAN MUSEUM IN
CAIRO. ABOVE WE SEE THE DETAIL OF THE PUNTITES WELCOMING THE
EGYPTIAN EXPEDITION. ABOVE THE DONKEY WE READ "THE DONKEY THAT
WILL CARRY HIS [KING OF PUNT] WIFE." BELOW, TWO PUNTITES CARRY
BAGS OF PRODUCE FROM THEIR LANDS, TO BE LOADED ONTO EGYPTIAN
VESSELS (EGYPTIAN MUSEUM, CAIRO).

162-163 PAREHU, KING OF PUNT, WITH HIS WIFE ITY AND THEIR
CHILDREN, WELCOMES THE CHIEF OF THE EGYPTIAN EXPEDITION, NEHESI,
AND HIS ENTOURAGE. THE QUEEN OF PUNT, PRECEDED BY HER HUSBAND,
IS SHOWN HERE WITH THE STEATOPYGIA TYPICAL OF WOMEN FROM
SEVERAL AFRICAN POPULATIONS (EGYPTIAN MUSEUM, CAIRO).

164 THIS DETAIL OF THE EXPEDITION TO PUNT FOCUSES ON THE STERN OF AN
EGYPTIAN SHIP AT THE TIME OF ARRIVAL. WE CAN SEE THE PROW AND STERN
SHAPED LIKE OPEN PAPYRUSES, THE DOUBLE-OAR HELM AND PART OF THE SAIL
BEING MANEUVERED BY THE CREW.

165 TOP ON THE SOUTHERN WALL OF THE PUNT PORTICO WE SEE A SCENE
THAT SHOWS PART OF AN EXOTIC LANDSCAPE, FEATURING THE *DUM* PALM AND
INCENSE TREES.

165 BOTTOM A STUDY UNDERTAKEN BY A TEAM OF ICHTHYOLOGISTS REVEALED
THAT THE AQUATIC HABITAT SHOWN ON THE WALLS OF THE PUNT PORTICO CAN
BE IDENTIFIED AS BEING PARTLY TYPICAL OF THE NILE, PARTLY THE RED SEA,
BUT ALSO THE INDIAN OCEAN.

166 TOP AND 167 IN THESE VIEWS OF THE TEMPLE OF AMUN-RE AT KARNAK, FROM THE SACRED LAKE AND THE AIR, WE CAN SEE THE OBELISKS OF THUTMOSIS I AND HATSHEPSUT.

166 BOTTOM THE IMAGE, ETCHED ONTO A QUARTZITE BLOCK, COMES FROM THE RED CHAPEL AND SHOWS A STANDING HATSHEPSUT, WITH A DOUBLE CROWN, AS SHE DEDICATES A PAIR OF OBELISKS TO THE GOD AMUN (LUXOR MUSEUM).

Hatshepsut's construction activities were not limited, however, to the House of Millions of Years on the west bank of Thebes. On the east bank, to commemorate her Jubilee, celebrated around the 16th year of her reign, she built two obelisks in front of the main entrance of the Temple of Karnak (only one of which is still in situ); in the central area of the temple itself she built a complex, at the center of which a splendid boat shrine for the god Amun was built in pink quartz (called the Red Chapel). The decoration of the chapel was completed later by Thutmosis III. Hatshepsut also inaugurated the north wing of the Temple of Karnak, constructing the 8th Pillar. Lastly, in the eastern part, Hatshepsut began the building of a new sanctuary dedicated to the sun god, also completed, as mentioned above, with two obelisks, today unfortunately no longer in existence.

Again on the east bank, Hatshepsut built a series of stopping places for Amun's boat, to be used during processions on feast days. Apart from Thebes, in Middle Egypt the queen had the rupestrian temple *(Speos Artemidos)* built, dedicated to the lioness goddess Pakhet, which the Hyksos had plundered and destroyed, according to the inscription engraved on the façade. The queen's name is present, however, even in sacred buildings in Elephantine, Cusae, Kom Ombo, al-Kab; while in Nubia her activities are documented in Sai, Qasr Ibrim, and in Buhen.

Like all pharaohs, Hatshepsut chose a group of trusted aides, some of whom had already served the crown during her predecessor's reign, and others who continued to hold their positions after the queen's death. As well as Hapuseneb, High Priest of Amun, who directed many works in Karnak, Hatshepsut availed herself of the help of two viziers, Ahmosi and User: we know that Nehesi directed the famous expedition to the country of Punt, while Amenhotep directed the organization of the Royal Jubilee. But the real right arm of the queen, the closest and most faithful aide was, for a large part of her reign, Senenmut, a man who lacked noble origins; he came from the ranks of the army. During Hatshepsut's reign, Senenmut acquired a long list of titles, roles, and privileges.

His career had begun during the reign of Thutmosis II, probably introduced at court by his mother, who could have served Queen Ahmose. Firstly, Senenmut was Steward of Hatshepsut's possessions, subsequently Steward of the Dominion of Amun, and he was also Superintendent of the Two Granaries (north and south), Priest of the Divine Boat of Amun, as well as Director of all the Royal Works. One of the most common images of the functionary depicts him as tutor to Neferure, Hatshepsut's daughter. The prestige and great respect he obviously enjoyed are testified by the large number of monuments in his name, as well as statues with splendid workmanship. Senenmut had two tombs built for himself – the second of which was famous for its astronomical ceiling – inside the city walls of *Djeser Djeseru*, and a chapel in Gebel Silsila, situated to the south of Thebes.

Nonetheless, his most audacious move was that of having himself depicted inside the queen's temple, in the most intimate quarters, where Amun was worshipped and where the funerary cult, dedicated to Thutmosis I and Hatshepsut herself, was observed. His image however, was wisely drawn at the end of the walls, close to the entrance so that the doors concealed it, when they were open. Senenmut probably died in about the 16th year of Hatshepsut's reign, because this is the last known date when he is mentioned, from an inscription on a vase in his unfinished tomb in Deir al-Bahari. Neferure, the queen's daughter, probably also died during this period.

The last inscription, which names Hatshepsut together with Thutmosis III, found in the Sinai, dates back to the 20th year of her reign, while the first image of the sovereign alone is dated in the 22nd year of her reign and is found on a stele located in the temple of Armant: this was the period when Hatshepsut died. Her body should have been buried in a tomb in the Valley of the Kings, which she had had built for herself (in fact, in the opinion of several scholars, extending KV 20, the tomb of her father) after her coronation, but both this and her previous tomb, pre-pared for her as Great Royal Wife, in a *wadi* between the Valley of the Queens and the Valley of the Kings, were found empty.

The disappearance of the Queen's corpse from the tomb, the absence of her name from regal lists, the fact that many of her images and cartouches had been can-celled (the latter were almost always substituted with the names of Thutmosis I or II) have led researchers to conclude that Hatshepsut must have suffered signifi-cant persecution after her death, instigated to cancel the memory of her existence from Egyptian history. Initially, Egyptologists supposed that the author of this *damnatio memoriae* could have been none other than Thutmosis III, who had been denied the throne for 15 years. Today there has been a partial rethinking of this theory and it is now thought that the first cancellations did not take place before the 42nd year of the reign of Thutmosis III. It is moreover agreed that most of the interventions occurred even later and in most cases were carried out by Ramesses II; indeed, numerous walls of the Deir al-Bahari temple bear a standard phrase, which says "King of Upper and Lower Egypt, Ramesses-Meri-Amun (Ramesses II) restored this monument for his father Amun-Re." The restoration of the famous Ramesside Pharaoh would have involved the restoration of all the names of the god Amun can-celled during the Amarna period.

168 THIS EROTIC SCENE, SKETCHED ON A ROCK INSIDE A NICHE TO THE NORTH OF THE UPPER TERRACE IN THE TEMPLE OF HATSHEPSUT AT DEIR AL-BAHARI, HAS BEEN INTERPRETED BY SOME AS A POLITICAL PARODY OF THE QUEEN AND HER COLLABORATOR SENENMUT.

169 THE RED QUARTZITE SCULPTURE PORTRAYS A KNEELING SENENMUT, ARCHITECT AND CLOSE COLLABORATOR OF HATSHEPSUT, HOLDING A LARGE COIL OF MEASURING TAPE, SYMBOLIZING HIS PROFESSION (THE LOUVRE, PARIS).

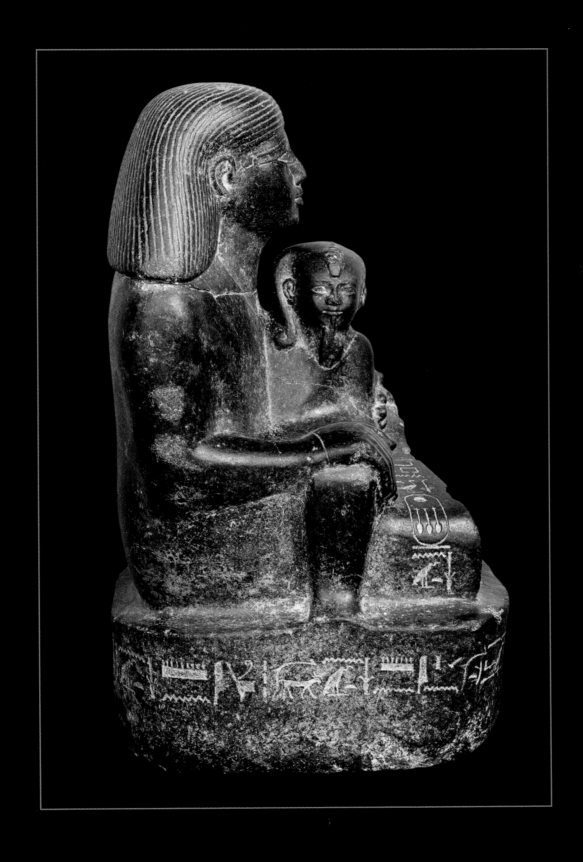

170 AND 171 THE MANY DUTIES OF SENENMUT INCLUDED BEING PRECEPTOR FOR HATSHEPSUT'S
DAUGHTER, NEFERURE. THIS SCULPTURE SHOWS THE FUNCTIONARY IN AN ATTITUDE NORMALLY
ASSOCIATED WITH A NURSE, EMBRACING THE HEIR TO THE THRONE: NEFERURE HAS THE PLAIT OF
CHILDHOOD AND THE *URAEUS* (EGYPTIAN MUSEUM, CAIRO).

172 THE DELICATE FACIAL FEATURES OF THIS COLOSSUS BETRAY THE FACT THAT HATSHEPSUT WAS REALLY A WOMAN (EGYPTIAN MUSEUM, CAIRO).

173 ZAHI HAWASS (LEFT) OBSERVES TWO FEMALE MUMMIES, ONE OF THE WET NURSE SATRE-IN AND ONE RECENTLY ATTRIBUTED TO HATSHEPSUT. THE IMAGE RIGHT REFERS TO WHAT IS PROBABLY THE MUMMY OF HATSHEPSUT WHICH, UNTIL 2006, WAS IN A TOMB IN THE VALLEY OF THE KINGS (KV 60) THAT BELONGED TO THE QUEEN'S WET NURSE. BELOW WE SEE THE X-RAY PROFILE OF THE MUMMY OF HATSHEPSUT. THE MISSING MOLAR WAS FOUND IN A CANOPIC VASE, INSCRIBED WITH THE QUEEN'S NAME, IN HER TEMPLE AT DEIR AL-BAHARI.

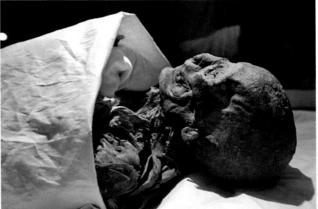

Despite the firm intentions of successors to "wipe out" Hatshepsut from Egyptian history, unceasing work by Egyptologists, now supported by the application of modern technologies, is providing increasingly solid contours of the existence and *post mortem* fate of the queen. In fact, in June 2007, Zahi Hawass, Secretary General of the Supreme Council of Egyptian Antiquities, called a press conference to announce that Hatshepsut's mummy had been identified. Remains of organs and a molar, contained in a canopic vase bearing her name, were compared with several – as yet unidentified – female mummies. The molar, in particular, was found to be compatible with a the dental arch of a woman whose body was buried in the ground and lacked any ornaments, and which has remained in the Valley of the Kings tomb (KV 60) where Howard Carter had found it in 1903. Further investigations, based chiefly on a comparison of this mummy's DNA with that of Hatshepsut's father, Thutmosis I, will be able to confirm this fascinating theory in the near future.

Notwithstanding the numerous innovations introduced in royal architecture even during the reign of Thutmosis III as sole ruler, the successors to Hatshepsut recovered almost all the themes present in *Djeser Djeseru* in their monuments: the axis of the temple was split, so that an east-west aspect, linked to the passage of the sun during the day, was integrated with an additional and important south-north axis, connected to the eternal succession of death and rebirth, expressed by the complementary nature of Osiris and Re; the definition of the divine nature of the sovereign through the representation of the carnal link with god the creator; the narration of the most significant events of her own reign, in order to demonstrate its substantial uniqueness. "Never before had anything similar been done by a King of Upper or Lower Egypt since the origins of time" is one of the expressions which would become recurrent on the regal monuments throughout the New Kingdom.

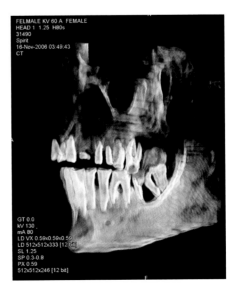

174 Lavish grave goods came to light in the almost intact tomb of Yuya and Tuya, parents of Queen Tiye. The mother's grave goods included several well-crafted *ushabty* and a casket, in inlaid gilded wood, which must have contained jewels stolen in ancient times (Egyptian Museum, Cairo).

175 The funeral mask in gilt cartonnage belongs to Tuya, mother of Tiye and thus the "mother-in-law" of Amenhotep III (Egyptian Museum, Cairo).

176-177 This small ebony sculpture, found in Medinet Gurob, portrays Queen Tiye with an expression that is profoundly different from traditional royal portraiture (Egyptian Museum, Berlin).

If the first two-thirds of the 18th Dynasty were characterized by a number of queens with a strong personality, the last third, including, among others, the reigns of Amenhotep III and his son Amenhotep IV, was literally crowded with female figures, constantly at the pharaoh's side in all his apparitions and activities. We have already mentioned the phenomenon of an assimilation of the roles of female deities to those of the queens, and the special relationship established in the

New Kingdom between the queen and the two daughters of Re, the goddesses Maat and Hathor. However, both on the walls of private tombs and on regal monuments, the sovereign ensured that she was often portrayed, not only with her two companions, but also with a number of princesses. Consequently, Tiye, Nefertiti, and Nefertari are often next to two other female figures of whom we do not always know the names and destiny. Let us proceed in order.

Amenhotep III made Tiye, a woman who was born in Akhmim in Middle Egypt and who did not have royal blood, his Great Royal Wife. She was the daughter of Yuya, priest of the god Min and Superintendent of the King's Horses, and Tuya, Superior in the Harem of Min.

Notwithstanding her non-aristocratic origins, the influence she had on her consort and the importance of the role assigned to her in the organization of power are documented from the beginning by numerous royal texts, among which was a series of scarabs, on which Amenhotep III had inscribed the most important events of his reign. On more than one occasion, scarabs were issued to commemorate events linked to Tiye, starting probably from the marriage. The fact is even more significant if we consider that marriage for the Egyptians held no social value in itself and was never celebrated as a particular event: the union between a man and a woman took on real value only when the union produced children. The phenomenon is even more relevant if we consider that the scarab inscription (4 inches/10.1 cm long) also mentioned the names of the Queen Tiye's parents, despite their non-aristocratic origins. A second series of scarabs, issued in the 11th year of the reign, gave news of a sacred lake dug close to the city of Akhmim, in honor of the queen. The day of the inauguration, the sovereigns sailed on the waters in a ship with the significant name of "Aten shines."

The sacred boat and the queen herself were therefore connected with a deity, the sun disc, which was to be crucial during the reign of Amenhotep III's successor. As well as the symbolic value, this lake also met a practical need, as it was actually a reservoir intended to channel water into a series of canals and allow more efficient irrigation of the surrounding area. The fact that this area was in the region of Tiye's city of origin gives us an idea of the great respect that the queen commanded, also demonstrated by official documents, where often we find a formula in which she appears to be associated with the throne of her consort: "Under the Majesty of the King of Upper and Lower Egypt, Amenhotep III and the Great Royal Wife, Tiye." Even so, notwithstanding her central role during the whole reign of Amenhotep III, Tiye was also the first Great Royal Wife to be flanked by another queen of the same rank, her daughter Sitamun, while other princesses, also daughters of the royal couple, are present on official monuments together with their parents and at least one more is defined as the Wife of the King.

The prestige which Tiye enjoyed is in any case testified by monumental evidence: a gigantic statue group (from Medinet Habu and now in the Egyptian Museum in Cairo), which portrays her sitting with the pharaoh, depicts the two sovereigns with the same dimensions. There are numerous images of Tiye in the Nubian temples of Soleb and Sedeinga, the latter dedicated to the queen and called The Temple of Tiye, as well as in the tombs of some functionaries of the reign. The fact that in one case it is a tomb in Tell al-Amarna gives the impression that the queen must have lived there for some time, certainly after the death of her consort, in memory of whom she had a series of scarabs engraved.

At least up to the 8th year of the reign of her son, Amenhotep IV, the image of Tiye is present even on Amarnian documents, while we know very little about her burial: her *shabti* were found in the tomb of Amenhotep II, whereas a royal sarcophagus with her name came from a Tell al-Amarna tomb and a golden *naos* from so-called Tomb 55 in the Valley of the Kings.

178 The life-size statue probably portrays Queen Tiye, using the traditional iconography of the Great Royal Wives. It was found in 2006 during excavation of the most recent foundations of the temple of Mut at Karnak (Egyptian Museum, Cairo).

178-179 The fragment of quartzite slab comes from the Temple of a Million Years, of Amenhotep III, in West Thebes. It depicts his wife, Tiye, in bas-relief in the hollow. The modeling of the face and the elongated eyes are a harbinger of Amarna art (Egyptian Museum, Berlin).

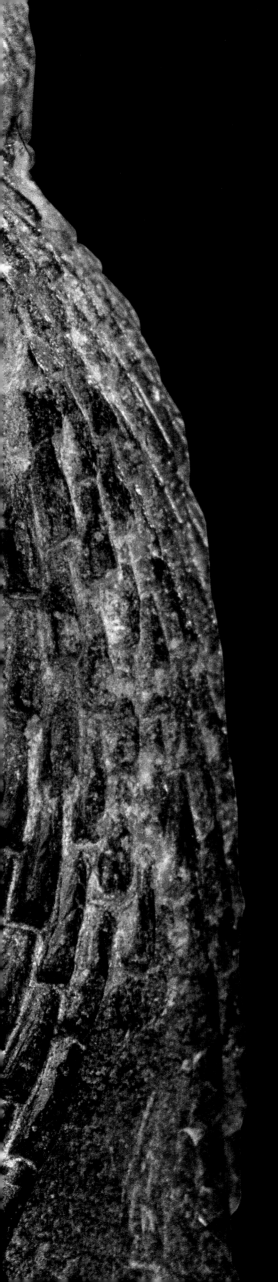

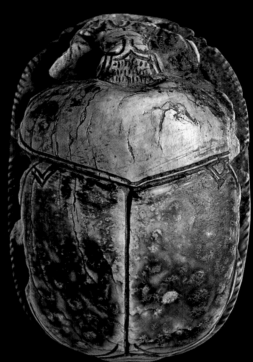

180-181 THE HEAD COMES FROM A SOAPSTONE STATUE OF TIYE,
FOUND BY SIR FLINDERS PETRIE IN 1905 AT SERABIT AL-KHADIM,
IN THE TEMPLE OF HATHOR, LADY OF TURQUOISE
(EGYPTIAN MUSEUM, CAIRO).

181 THE FIRST 12 YEARS OF AMENHOTEP III'S VERY LONG REIGN
WERE CHARACTERIZED BY THE ISSUE OF FIVE SERIES OF SCARABS,
EACH COMMEMORATING A PARTICULAR EVENT. THE ISSUE IN THE
SECOND YEAR, THE PERIOD OF THIS SCARAB IN ENAMELED SCHIST,
COMMEMORATES THE "MARRIAGE" OF THE PHARAOH WITH QUEEN
TIYE (THE LOUVRE, PARIS).

182-183 THE SCENE SHOWS STATUES OF AMENHOTEP III AND
TIYE BEING MOVED ON SLEDS, IN RAMESSIDE TOMB TT 277.
THE SCULPTURES OF THE DEIFIED SOVEREIGNS ARE ACCOMPANIED
BY VARIOUS PRIESTS.

Even in the singular history of the reign of Amenhotep IV, female figures appear fundamental and again in this case, the chief queen, Nefertiti is supported by another Great Royal Wife, as well as by a series of princesses, frequently portrayed together with the royal couple.

Nothing is known about the family of Nefertiti, nor do we know her parents' names but as his father did with his mother, Amenhotep IV seemed not to care about the non-aristocratic origins of his wife, and together they took another step forward in the development of the new solar theology that was being established during the 18th Dynasty: the only god was Aten, the sun disc, and the only intermediaries between the divine world and men were the pharaoh and his family.

The phenomenon, known as the "religious revolution" or "Amarnian Heresy" distorted, for about twenty years, culture, traditions, art, and pharaonic society: everything that was there before was set aside by such a strong wave of innovation that the Egyptians could not accept it. The queen, or rather the queens, who supported the pharaoh in this undertaking were involved in extraordinary representative roles: one of the newer aspects is the sensation of movement perceived in the royal images, not only in the human figures but also the dress and the ribbons that decorate them, which seem to be in constant movement. Themes that cannot be reconciled with the hieratic character of the royal family were introduced into the figurative program of the monuments: numerous scenes portray the royal family's intimate moments.

Amenhotep (who changed his own name to Akhenaten, "He who is useful to Aten") and his wife Nefertiti (whose second name is Neferneferuaten "Perfect is the perfection of Aten") are shown in front of each other with their children (all girls) playing in their laps or all together mourning the death of one of the princesses.

The queen was also portrayed in positions which had previously been reserved for the reigning sovereign: as well as carrying out rituals and celebrating the cult – alone or accompanied by one of her daughters – Nefertiti is depicted driving her own racing chariot, or in the traditional iconography of the pharaoh striking the enemy and holding him by the hair. More even than Tiye and Hatshepsut, Nefertiti became the female counterpart of royalty, a perfectly complementary figure to that of her husband.

Nefertiti, like Tiye, was also commemorated with many monuments because, as we mentioned, her presence was constant alongside the sovereign. As well as relief work and statue groups which portray her with Akhenaten, the queen was also portrayed in many in-the-round sculptures, including a splendid bust worthy of note and found by archaeologists in the study of the court sculptor, Thutmosis in Tell al-Amarna, now in in Berlin's Altes Museum. However, nothing is known about her burial and her mummy, notwithstanding the many theories expounded, some of which are rather improbable, even suggesting that Nefertiti did not die during Akhenaten's reign but that she continued to rule in Egypt for some time under the name of Smenkhare.

186-187 The seductive face of
Nefertiti is characterized by a
realism and a simultaneous purity of
feature that have few equals in
Egyptian art. This close-up shows the
delicate curves of her chin, mouth
and eyes (Egyptian Museum, Berlin).

188 Ludwig Borchardt, director of
the 1912 German excavations at Tell
al-Amarna, sought at length but in
vain to find the other rock crystal
setting missing from the left eye of
the portrait of Nefertiti (Egyptian
Museum, Berlin).

189 The image of the reverse of the
Nefertiti bust shows the presence of
a red ribbon between her shoulders.
Paintings and bas-reliefs of the
period render this ribbon with
undulating lines that give the
Amarnian images their unique sense
of dynamism (Egyptian Museum,
Berlin).

190 and 191 Although incomplete,
this quartzite head of Nefertiti also
reveals the sensitivity and ability of
Thutmosis, one of the great artists
of the New Kingdom.
The face shows the black strokes of
several details (Egyptian Museum,
Cairo).

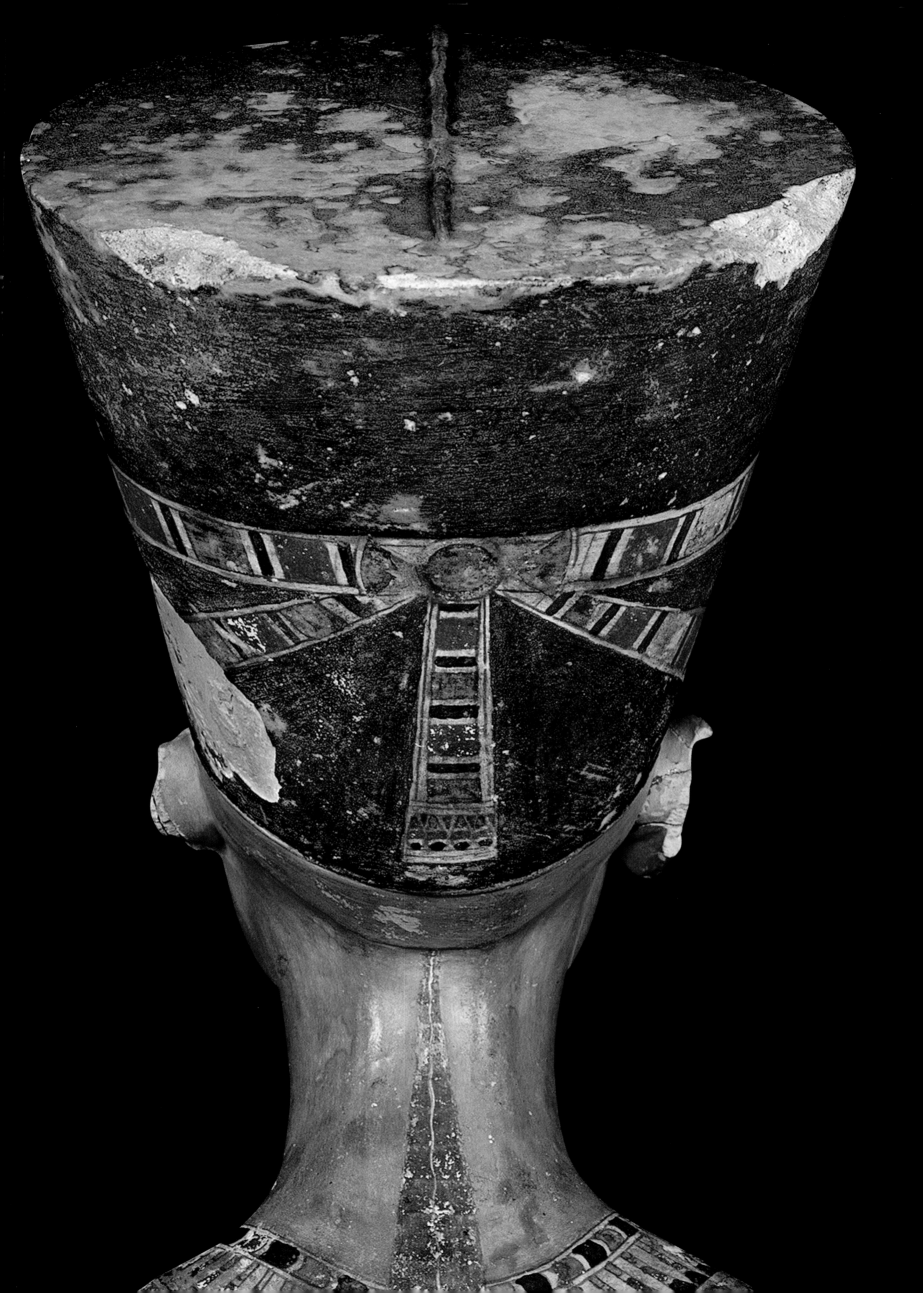

192 THE SMALL SCULPTED GROUP,
IN PAINTED LIMESTONE, SHOWS
AKHENATEN WITH NEFERTITI,
APPLYING THE PRECEPTS OF AMARNA
ART. SOME OF THE MOST EVIDENT
ASPECTS ARE THE LACK OF RIGIDITY,
THE ALMOST DEFORMED LINES OF
THE PROFILES, AND
THE RESEMBLANCE BETWEEN
THE MALE AND FEMALE BODIES
(THE LOUVRE, PARIS).

193 THE CURVING CONTOURS OF
THE FIGURES, THE MOVEMENTS
IMPLICIT ON THE ARTICULATIONS OF
THE LIMBS, THE SOFTLY DRAPED
GARMENTS, CHARACTERIZING
FIGURATIVE ART IN THE AMARNA
PERIOD, ARE EASY TO SEE IN THIS
PERSPECTIVE OF THE SCULPTED
GROUP OF AKHENATEN AND
NEFERTITI (THE LOUVRE, PARIS).

194-195 The fragment of a head in polished yellow jasper, purchased by E.S. Harkness to the Metropolitan Museum of Art in New York in 1926, must have been part of a composite statue, probably with a calcite body. Despite the huge gaps in the relic, the facial features and the shape of the mouth allow us to identify it as the portrait of an Amarnian queen (Metropolitan Museum of Art, New York).

195 The slab, with bas-relief carving in the hollow, shows Akhenaten, alongside his wife and children, making offerings to Aten. The single god of the Amarnian religion has abandoned the anthropomorphism of traditional Egyptian divinities, except for the extension of rays into the shape of hands (Egyptian Museum, Cairo).

196-197 Akhenaten and Nefertiti are shown with three daughters in a scene of familial intimacy, typical of the period's figurative art. There is also a significant and exclusive presence of female figures next to the pharaoh (Egyptian Museum, Berlin).

198 Sports, especially archery, are one of the subjects of image repertoires in the royal monuments of the New Kingdom. This example comes from one of the walls of the casket of Tutankhamun; it shows Queen Ankhesenamun at the feet of the pharaoh as he prepares to shoot an arrow (Egyptian Museum, Cairo).

199 One surface of a casket, from the grave goods of Tutankhamun, is decorated with a bucolic scene. In a context literally teeming with flowers, Ankhesenamun offers two large bouquets to her groom. At the base of the scene there are two female figures depicted picking flowers (Egyptian Museum, Cairo).

After the death of Akhenaten, whose body was never found, his successor restored Thebes as the capital and reinstated traditional cults, attempting to cancel completely the memory of his predecessor's existence, although he was not wholly successful. Nevertheless, the art and thought of the post-Amarna period reflect the novelties introduced by Akhenaten, in both style and subject. Moreover, his immediate successors had blood ties with him, even if we are not sure of their exact nature: one of the most plausible theories is that Smenkhare, Ay, Tutankhamun, and Horemheb were related to the reigning house through marriages with royal princesses; but some experts contend that at least Smenkhare and Tutankhamun could be Akhenaten's own children.

200 TUTANKHAMUN AND ANKHESENAMUN ARE SHOWN IN AN AFFECTIONATE POSE AS THE QUEEN RUBS
SCENTED UNGUENT ON HER HUSBAND. THE SCENE IS EMBOSSED ONTO THE BACKREST OF THE
PHARAOH'S THRONE, FOUND AMONGST THE SURVIVING GRAVE GOODS IN HIS TOMB (KV 62). THE
WOODEN THRONE IS DECORATED IN GOLD LEAF WITH INLAID HARDSTONES AND POLYCHROMATIC
ENAMELS (EGYPTIAN MUSEUM, CAIRO).

201 THE SHUTTERS OF THE FRONT PANEL ON THIS STATUE SHRINE, FOUND AMONG THE GRAVE GOODS
OF TUTANKHAMUN, SHOW SIX SCENES IN WHICH QUEEN ANKHESENAMUN OFFERS THE SOVEREIGN
VARIOUS RITUAL ITEMS (EGYPTIAN MUSEUM, CAIRO).

202-203 The important role of queens in the New Kingdom is emphasized by the frequency with which the royal wives are shown with their husbands. This detail from the backrest of Tutankhamun's gold throne shows Queen Ankhesenamun (Egyptian Museum, Cairo).

204-205 The scenes embossed onto the gold shrine, part of Tutankhamun's grave goods, include a sporting image of the young pharaoh, depicted as he shoots an arrow. The sovereign, shown with a panther, is in the company of his wife (Egyptian Museum, Cairo).

The events of the closing years of the 18th Dynasty are, in any case, rather confused and we must wait until the reign of Ramesses II to be able to see another great queen. Nefertari Merimut was a Great Royal Wife and Lady of the Two Lands but, like Tiye and Nefertiti, she was not God's Wife of Amun, an epithet which was added to her titles in a later moment. We do not have definite information about her origins but it has been suggested that she descended from the family of Ay, one of Akhenaten's successors. Nefertari married Ramesses when he had not yet succeeded to the throne and died before the Jubilee of the 30th year of his reign. On the basis of textual documentation, it would appear that she gave the pharaoh six of his many children, of whom two were girls, who became Great Royal Wives upon the death of their mother.

There are similarities between some aspects of the characters (from what can be reconstructed through the official documents): the iconography and titulary of Nefertari recall Queen Tiye. This should not be a surprise if we consider, as already mentioned, that many of Ramesses II's decisions clearly manifest the desire to emulate his illustrious ancestor Amenhotep III, who in the royal Ramesside lists appears as the last sovereign of the 18th Dynasty before Horemheb.

Right from the beginning of her spouse's reign, Nefertari participated in main state events. The scenes engraved on the temple walls portray her during ceremonies and celebrating religious feasts, but she also seems to have had an important role in foreign policy. During the reign of Ramesses II there was a fierce battle between the Hittites and the Egyptians, fought on the River Orontes, close to the city of Qadesh.

Notwithstanding the official texts produced by both sides – and Ramesses, in particular, gave great importance to this conflict which he had portrayed on several of his monuments – the battle did not succeed in ratifying the supremacy of either of the two great powers. Thus, a few years later, a bilateral peace treaty was signed, preceded, as can well be imagined, by intense diplomatic activity, in which Nefertari herself participated. Indeed she began a correspondence with Pudukhepa, the wife of the Hittite sovereign, with whom she also exchanged gifts. The result was a long period of peace, well-being and relative calm on the borders of the Egyptian Empire.

207 THIS DETAIL OF THE PORTRAIT OF NEFERTARI COMES FROM HER TOMB
IN THE VALLEY OF THE QUEENS. THE SOVEREIGN WEARS A WIG WITH
PRECIOUS GOLD DECORATIONS AT THE BASE OF THE LOCKS OF HAIR, AND A
PAIR OF EARRINGS THAT REPRODUCE THE URAEUS. A HEAVY, FIVE-STRAND
NECKLACE ENLIVENS THE WHITE PLEATED TUNIC.

Two monuments, both of great importance, remain as evidence of the important role and the significant prestige enjoyed by Nefertari: the so-called minor temple of Abu Simbel and her splendid tomb in the Valley of the Queens (QV 66).

At Abu Simbel in Nubia, Ramesses had two temples built, one dedicated to his own *ka* and the principal male deities of his reign: Re, Amun, and Ptah; the second was dedicated to his wife, likened to the goddess Hathor. Inside this temple, the queen is portrayed as she presents offerings of flowers and sistrums to the great goddesses Isis, Hathor, and Mut, receiving a sort of investiture in exchange, during which she was decorated with the same symbols as the divine wives of Amun.

208 Here we see the detail of one of the colossi that decorate the façade of the great temple of Abu Simbel. Beside the legs of the seated Ramesses II, there is a high-relief sculpture of the Great Royal Wife, Nefertari.

208-209 THE IMAGE IS AN OVERVIEW OF THE TWO TEMPLES OF ABU SIMBEL. IN THE BACKGROUND THE GREAT TEMPLE DEDICATED TO THE GOD AMUN; IN THE FOREGROUND THE SMALL TEMPLE, DEDICATED TO THE GODDESS HATHOR AND TO QUEEN NEFERTARI, IDENTIFIED WITH THE GODDESS.

210-211 THE FAÇADE OF THE SMALL TEMPLE OF ABU SIMBEL BEARS THE COLOSSI OF NEFERTARI AND HER HUSBAND. THE ICONOGRAPHY OF THE QUEEN, WITH HORNS, SUN DISK, AND DOUBLE FEATHERS, MAKES HER IMMEDIATELY ASSIMILABLE TO THE GODDESS HATHOR.

212-213 This is a view of the axial corridor through the hypostyle hall of the Small Temple of Abu Simbel. On the sides of the pillars not only Nefertari and Ramesses II are depicted, but also various deities. In the *naos*, which opens into the rear wall, there is a zoomorphic statue of the goddess Hathor.

214 Along the axial corridor, the pillars in the hypostyle hall of the Small Temple are decorated with a Hathoric sistrum, whose "handle" is inscribed with a formula of offerings; two side columns bear the cartouches of Ramesses II and Nefertari.

215 Inside the Small Temple, Queen Nefertari is frequently portrayed with the Hathoric sistrum and a bouquet of flowers. Her forehead is decorated with the Hathoric uraeus and the head of the vulture.

216 QUEEN NEFERTARI IS PORTRAYED ON A WALL OF THE SMALL TEMPLE OF ABU SIMBEL, IN THE ACT OF OFFERING A SISTRUM AND A BOUQUET OF FLOWERS TO THE GODDESS ANUKIS, A DIVINITY OF UPPER EGYPT, CHARACTERIZED BY A TALL TAPERING HAT MADE OF RUSH STEMS TIED AT THE BASE.

217 QUEEN NEFERTARI OFFERS TWO SISTRUMS TO THE GODDESS HATHOR, "LADY OF THE HEAVENS, PRINCESS OF ALL GODS." THE QUEEN WEARS A BAG WIG AND THE USUAL EMBLEMS, AND UNLIKE THE GODDESS, AN AMPLE PLEATED TUNIC.

Over recent years, following a long period of closure to the public as restoration work could no longer be delayed, tomb QV 66 has become one of the most desirable destinations for visitors going to the royal necropolises in West Thebes.

The monument underwent a first restoration in 1986, managed by the Egyptian Organization of Antiquities (now Supreme Council of Antiquities), partnering the Getty Conservation Institute. The operation allowed salvaging of several sections of the decoration, which appeared to be in extremely precarious conditions; a second, conclusive intervention was undertaken from 1988 to 1994, by a team of restorers led by Paolo Mora, and this involved all the hypogeum walls as well as enabling the restoration of one of the most original masterpieces of the New Kingdom.

In 1904, during the second excavation campaign in the Valley of the Queens, Ernesto Schiaparelli, director of the Egyptian Museum of Turin, discovered the queen's tomb and immediately realized that he was looking at

one of the most refined burial monuments of the Theban period. In the distant past, however, the tomb had been almost completely ransacked, so Schiaparelli found only the sarcophagus lid, a few grave-goods and part of the queen's mummy, now on display in the Egyptian Museum of Turin.

The hypogeum is 92 ft (28 m) in length and was excavated from a layer of very crumbly porous rock, at about 26 ft (8 m) below ground.

While these conditions caused the painted walls to suffer continual infiltration of damp and the flooding that very occasionally affects the *wadis* of the Egyptian desert, they nonetheless forced craftsmen to choose techniques that made it possible to give the decoration features that made it

218 NEFERTARI IS PORTRAYED INSIDE HER TOMB IN FRONT OF THE GOD THOT AND ACCOMPANIED BY THE FALCON GOD HORUS.

218-219 THE IMAGE SHOWS AN OVERVIEW OF THE EASTERN WALL OF THE ANTECHAMBER OF NEFERTARI'S TOMB.

220-221 DETAIL OF A WALL IN NEFERTARI'S TOMB SUCCESSFULLY DEPICTS THE TRANSPARENCY OF THE QUEEN'S WHITE LINEN TUNIC, UNDER WHICH WE CAN SEE THE COLOR OF HER ARMS AND THE GOLD BANDS IN HER WIG.

one of the most extraordinary examples of Egyptian figurative art. The artists actually had to prime the walls with quite a thick layer of gypsum plaster, which assured a compact, luminous surface for decoration, which meant that the refined painting techniques of the time could be exploited to the full.

Thanks to the color contrast between the background and the depicted subjects, as well as the use of shading, the resulting visual effect is that of a bas-relief decoration characterized by great radiance and vitality.

The complex figurative and textual program falls into two complementary paths, along which the Nefertari's life-after-death would evolve.

The first develops along the tomb's main axis (south-north), from the antechamber to the Golden Room (or sarcophagus room), ending with the queen's transfiguration so she could be embraced by the gods. Subsequently, as shown in the paintings in the solar complex (set to the east of the antechamber), as a dweller in the Hereafter, Osiris-Nefertari could receive the food of the gods and enjoy the cyclical regeneration of her body by Re, the Sun god.

222 TOP THE GODDESS NEKHBET, IN THE GUISE OF A VULTURE, GUARDS THE ENTRANCE IN THE
VESTIBULE OF NEFERTARI'S TOMB BY SPREADING HER WINGS. THE GODDESS IS DEFINED AS "THE WHITE
ONE OF NEKHEN," THE TOWN IN SOUTHERN EGYPT WHERE SHE ORIGINATED.

222 BOTTOM THE FOUR SONS OF HORUS, IMSET, HAPY, DUAMUTEF, AND QEBEHSENUF, FOLLOWED BY
THE FALCON GOD HIMSELF, ARE DEPICTED ON THE DOOR LINTEL LEADING INTO THE ANTECHAMBER
WITH ACCESS TO THE RAMP DOWN INTO NEFERTARI'S TOMB. THE MAIN TASK OF THESE GODS WAS TO
PROTECT THE DECEASED'S INTERNAL ORGANS, PLACED IN CANOPIC VASES.

223 KHEPRI, ONE MANIFESTATION OF THE SUN GOD RE, IS DEPICTED WITH THE HEAD OF A SCARAB,
SYMBOL OF BECOMING AND THE HIEROGLYPH USED TO WRITE HIS NAME. HE STATES THAT HE CONCEDES
TO NEFERTARI, "ETERNITY LIKE RA ... AND A PLACE IN THE NECROPOLIS;" THE GOD IS DEFINED AS "HE
WHO IS IN HIS BOAT, THE GREAT GOD."

224-225 THE TWO GREAT FALCONS, IDENTIFIED AS NEPHTHYS AND ISIS, PROTECT THE BODY OF
NEFERTARI, ASSIMILATED TO OSIRIS, IN HER SARCOPHAGUS. THE TWO DIVINITIES, WHO ARE SISTERS AND
COMPANIONS OF THE GOD, ARE THE MAIN PLAYERS IN THE BURIAL RITUALS THAT LEAD TO THE

226 In funeral texts, the deceased's requests include that of being able to transform into a phoenix, the legendary bird from Eastern lands, linked to sun worship and considered to be the soul of Re; the main center of worship in Egypt was, in fact, Heliopolis. This detail comes from a wall in Nefertari's tomb (QV 66).

226-227 The image shows one of the two lions that support the *akhet* symbol, in other words the horizon: this is one of the numerous vignettes that accompany Chapter 17 of the Book of the Dead, on the west wall of the antechamber of Nefertari's tomb. The text, born as an expression of the solar theology, was then transformed into a chapter in favor of the deceased.

228-229 Queen Nefertari is portrayed — on the west wall of the ramp down to her tomb (QV 66) — as she presents offerings to the two female divinities: Hathor with horns and sun disk, and Selkis, the scorpion goddess, who grants eternity to Nefertari.

230 The burial chamber in the tomb of Nefertari presents a very complex decoration scheme, which illustrates the Afterworld: apart from Osiris, there are other divinities who welcome the queen.

231 Queen Nefertari offers precious fabrics to the mummiform god Ptah, depicted inside the gilded tabernacle, supported on the front of the *djed* pillars. The god is defined as "Lord of Truth, Sovereign of the Two Lands, handsome of Face on His Great Throne."

232 The jackal god Anubis welcomes Nefertari to her tomb. The queen
is defined "Beloved Daughter, Great Royal Bride,
Lady of the Two Lands."

233 The mummiform god Osiris is depicted on the axial corridor of the
pillars of the Room of Gold or room of the sarcophagus; he wears the
atef crown and, with his hands close to his chest, holds the *heqa*
scepter and the *nekhekh* whip. The god stands in a tabernacle and is
flanked by the symbols of Anubis.

234-235 In 1916, in a tomb without decorations, not far from Hatshepsut's first burial, local grave-robbers found the grave goods of the three foreign brides of Thutmosis III intact. This precious gold and inlaid wig cover was contained in one part of the grave goods (Metropolitan Museum of Art, New York).

235 To seal the peace treaty signed with the Hittite king, Hattusilis III, Ramesses II decided to marry the latter's daughter, who took the name of Maathorneferure. The two cuneiform panels contain the missives that the pharaoh sent to Pudukhepa, the wife of the Hittite king, to organize this marriage (Ankara Museum and Istanbul Museum).

We should remember several other female figures before we set aside the New Kingdom: foreign wives of the sovereigns. Some were sent to the pharaoh as a sign of submission, almost a tribute, others came to Egypt to ratify international agreements through a diplomatic marriage with the Egyptian sovereign. However, the opposite never occurred (at least not until after the end of the New Kingdom): an Egyptian princess was never given as a wife to a foreign sovereign, as is underlined in Amenhotep III's letter to a king of Babylon who had made the request "From the beginning, the daughter of an Egyptian king has never been given in matrimony to any (foreigner)."

From the little it is possible to reconstruct, on the basis of available documents, the status of these princesses cannot have been very high once they arrived in Egypt. In one case, the Babylonian King Kadamashman Enlil sent a letter to Amenhotep III asking for information about his own sister, from whom he had had no more news. It is more than likely that many of them (together with their slaves) were sent to work in production activities, especially textiles, while others could be assigned to the organization of the palaces belonging to the pharaoh. A single exception can be made with regard to this situation: one of the Hittite wives of Ramesses II, who on arriving in Egypt took an Egyptian name, Maathorneferure, and presumably acquired at her father's request the title Great Royal Wife.

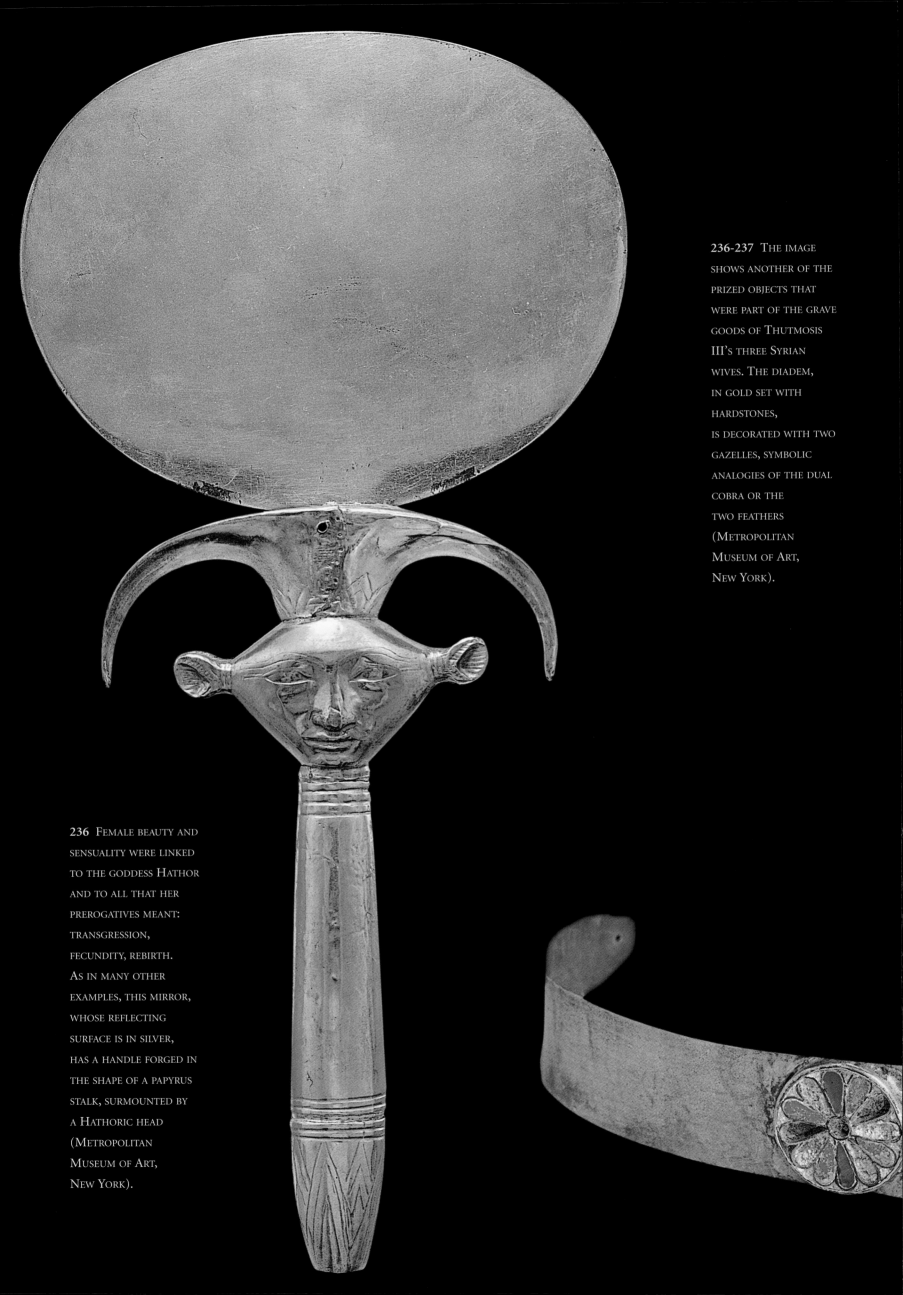

236-237 THE IMAGE
SHOWS ANOTHER OF THE
PRIZED OBJECTS THAT
WERE PART OF THE GRAVE
GOODS OF THUTMOSIS
III'S THREE SYRIAN
WIVES. THE DIADEM,
IN GOLD SET WITH
HARDSTONES,
IS DECORATED WITH TWO
GAZELLES, SYMBOLIC
ANALOGIES OF THE DUAL
COBRA OR THE
TWO FEATHERS
(METROPOLITAN
MUSEUM OF ART,
NEW YORK).

236 FEMALE BEAUTY AND
SENSUALITY WERE LINKED
TO THE GODDESS HATHOR
AND TO ALL THAT HER
PREROGATIVES MEANT:
TRANSGRESSION,
FECUNDITY, REBIRTH.
AS IN MANY OTHER
EXAMPLES, THIS MIRROR,
WHOSE REFLECTING
SURFACE IS IN SILVER,
HAS A HANDLE FORGED IN
THE SHAPE OF A PAPYRUS
STALK, SURMOUNTED BY
A HATHORIC HEAD
(METROPOLITAN
MUSEUM OF ART,
NEW YORK).

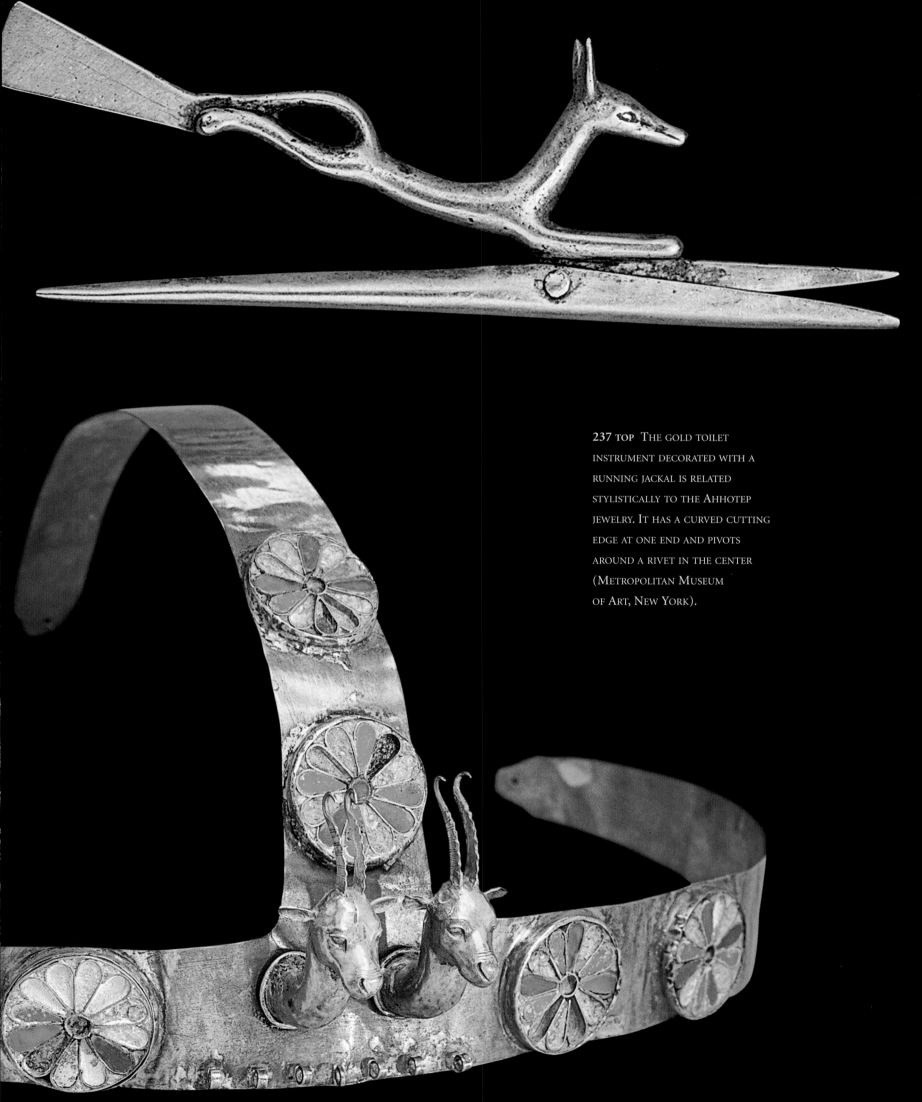

237 top The gold toilet instrument decorated with a running jackal is related stylistically to the Ahhotep jewelry. It has a curved cutting edge at one end and pivots around a rivet in the center (Metropolitan Museum of Art, New York).

THE LATE PERIOD

In the period immediately following the end of the New Kingdom, only the Divine Adoratrices of Amun had a role similar to that of the Royal Wives, at least apparently. Despite sharing many titles (Lady of the Two Lands and Lady of the Crowns) and royal prerogatives (dedicating religious buildings, celebrating divine rituals, commemorating the Jubilee), the role was mainly priestly, and even in this activity they were always supported by a Great Steward, whose power and prestige in Thebes was absolutely similar to that of a pharaoh. Moreover, from an ideological point of view, as virgins dedicated exclusively to the cult of Amun, the Divine Adoratrices no longer represented the royal family as the incarnation of the divine archetype on earth, but were a simple instrument in the hands of the god: they were priestesses, not queens.

The 700 years which separate the end of the New Kingdom from the beginning of the Ptolemaic period are characterized by a sequence of foreign sovereigns: Libyans, Nubians, and Persians who alternated on the throne of Egypt with the last local dynasties (26th, 28th, 29th, and 30th), later supplanted definitively when Alexander the Great conquered Egypt in 332 BC. It was only after Alexander's death, with the division of the huge empire among his satraps, that the Ptolemies (or Lagids) tried to reinstate the ancient concept of divine Egyptian royalty, reviving the traditional bipolarism based on the indivisible link between the pharaoh and his wife. It was no coincidence that in this phase of Egyptian history, and for the whole of the Graeco-Roman period, the female deity chosen to represent the queen was the goddess Isis.

239 LEFT THE CASKET LID IN
PAINTED WOOD WAS CREATED
IN THE FORM OF A CARTOUCHE
AND BEARS THE NAMES
OF NITOCRIS I, ACCOMPANIED
BY A PAIR OF URAEI
(THE LOUVRE, PARIS).

239 RIGHT THE SARCOPHAGUS
BELONGS TO NITOCRIS I,
DAUGHTER OF THE SAITIC
SOVEREIGN, PSAMMETICHUS I
(26TH DYNASTY) (EGYPTIAN
MUSEUM, CAIRO).

240 AND 241 AUGUSTE
MARIETTE WAS INSPIRED BY
THE DIVINE ADORATRICE
AMENIRDIS WHEN HE CREATED
THE CHARACTER OF AMNERIS
FOR AN OPERA THAT WAS TO BE
PERFORMED ON THE OCCASION
OF THE OPENING OF THE SUEZ
CANAL. TAKING MARIETTE'S
ORIGINAL IDEA, GIUSEPPE
VERDI AND THE LIBRETTIST
ANTONIO GHISLANZONI
WROTE *AIDA* (EGYPTIAN
MUSEUM, CAIRO).

CLEOPATRA AND THE PTOLEMAIC QUEENS

CHAPTER 4

The reign of sovereigns of Greek origin in Egypt is characterized by a definite desire to integrate, at least formally, with local customs, reviving a tradition that dated back to the great reigns of the pharaohs. This is clearly demonstrated by building activity dedicated to the local deities, by the fundamental role assigned to the Egyptian priests, who became, in some way, the intermediaries between the reigning dynasty and the population. It is further underlined by the decision to adopt titles and iconography, as well as celebrations and behavior, typical of the pharaohs, and most importantly the assimilation with the divine world.

Initially the Ptolemaic sovereigns were worshiped only at a local and spontaneous level. Ptolemy I founded the dynastic cult and in 280/279 BC he proclaimed the deification of his predecessor Ptolemy I Soter. At the same time, there was also a progressive transformation of the royal female figure, who tended to identify herself increasingly with Isis (and if necessary even with Hathor). A parallel change occurred in the titulary of the goddesses, who, in turn, acquired royal titles, such as Lady of the Two Lands, Female Sun, and Sovereign of Upper and Lower Egypt.

Arsinoe II, wife and sister of Ptolemy II Philadelphus (285–246 BC) appeared almost as a female pharaoh. Applying the rules of Egyptian tradition a titulary was established, which remained in use for other queens: Sovereign of the Two Lands, She Who Makes the King Delight and Whom the Gods Love, Daughter of Amun, Lady of the Diadems, Arsinoe, Who Loves Her Brother, She Who Delights the Heart of the Maat and Whom the Gods Love. Arsinoe also maintained the titulary after her death and thus came to identify herself totally with Isis, as sister and wife of the king of the dead.

With Ptolemy III and Berenice III, there is a further step forward in the transformation of the role of queens, now portrayed behind the king when celebrating the divine cult. Berenice also takes the title and name of Horus. Furthermore, in some demotic documents, she is depicted as the *per-aat*, that is the feminine of the Ancient Egyptian term *per-aa* meaning "pharaoh." In the case of Cleopatra I and Ptolemy V Epiphanes (205–180 BC), the royal couple was portrayed as "The pharaohs Ptolemy and Cleopatra" whereas Cleopatra II, wife of Ptolemy VI, was named "Female Sun."

242 This marble head probably depicts Arsinoe III, sister and wife of Ptolemy IV. Arsinoe was also the first Ptolemaic queen to conceive a son by her own brother (The Louvre, Paris).

244 The bas relief, of the Ptolemaic period, depicts a queen or possibly a female deity. The slab may be an *ex-voto* or a study for a sculpture (Egyptian Museum, Turin).

245 This statue of a queen, in painted limestone, is certainly datable to the Ptolemaic period, although it cannot be designated as being any specific sovereign. Nonetheless, it is interesting to note how the iconography has faithfully reproduced the dress and emblems of the Pharaonic period (Egyptian Museum, Cairo).

246 and 247 The head is thought to be of Cleopatra I, wife of Ptolemy V, or of Cleopatra II, wife of Ptolemy VI. The queen has a typically Greek hairstyle, but her head is decorated with the classic emblems of pharaonic regality (Alexandria Archaeological Museum).

248 and 249 The images show a marble head that depicts a Ptolemaic queen, assimilated with Isis, sister and wife of Osiris. The head is of uncertain identity and might be either Cleopatra II or her daughter, Cleopatra III (The Louvre, Paris).

250 ON THE WALLS OF THE KOM OMBO TEMPLE, PTOLEMY VI IS SHOWN WITH HIS OLDER SISTER AND
SECOND WIFE, CLEOPATRA II, AS HE PERFORMS THE OFFERING RITE. THE QUEEN'S HEAD IS DECORATED
WITH THE USUAL EMBLEMS OF FEMALE DEITIES AND QUEENS FROM THE NEW KINGDOM: URAEUS, HORN
WITH SUN DISK, AND DOUBLE FEATHERS.

251 BOTH THE SOVEREIGNS OF GREEK ORIGIN, THE PTOLEMIES, AND THE ROMAN EMPERORS, BUILT
TEMPLES IN EGYPT IN THE PHARAONIC STYLE, DEDICATED TO EGYPTIAN DEITIES. THIS BAS RELIEF,
ETCHED IN A COLUMN AT THE KOM OMBO TEMPLE, DEPICTS THE GODDESS ISIS-HATHOR,
WITH EMBLEMS OF THE MAIN FEMALE DEITIES OF PHARAONIC EGYPT.

But it was with Cleopatra (VII) Philopator, the most famous of the queens of Ptolemy, that we find the moment when a woman is depicted in the act of performing the pharaonic rite of the offering of the Maat. The complex and singular story, and Cleopatra's dramatic demise, reconstructed through the works of classical authors, such as Dio Cassius, Plutarch, and Pliny the Elder (to mention just a few), aroused such interest in scholars and in the general public that it generated enormous literary production, ranging from works of a scientific nature to legend, embracing tragedy and films. A (sadly) small number of documents must be added to the historical sources that have helped us to reconstruct Cleopatra's image, at least partially: as for the other Ptolemaic queens, some statues and the relief work on the temple walls dedicated to the Egyptian deities portray her in "pharaonic" style, while other sculptures and the coins show her portrait according to the Hellenistic style.

The events that characterize Cleopatra's reign start with her succession to the throne in 51 BC, with the death of her father, Ptolemy XII. She married her brother Ptolemy XIII, in compliance with their father's will and in accordance with a rigid dynastic rule. Given the young age of her brother, who was only about ten, Cleopatra assumed full responsibility for ruling the country at a particularly complex time. In addition to domestic problems (a discontented peasantry, brought to its knees by famine; hostility of other members of her own family), there were problematic foreign relations, above all because of Rome's growing demands for taxes. A series of intelligent decisions, regarding both economic and religious policy, enabled her to regain the trust of the country and to begin an important phase of recovery. Unfortunately, in 48 BC the hostility of her husband and brother, supported by some advisors, forced Cleopatra to abandon Egypt and take refuge on the eastern border, in Syria. Julius Caesar intervened to restore Cleopatra to her father's throne and re-establish some sort of peace between Cleopatra and her consort. Caesar remained in Alexandria for a long period, during which he became Cleopatra's companion, not only in ruling the country but also in her private life. A new attempt by Ptolemy XIII to eliminate her and to regain control of power ended in a bloody battle, during which Ptolemy himself died.

Respecting tradition, Cleopatra married her other brother, Ptolemy XIV, but it was with Caesar that she took a long journey down the Nile, with the double objective of presenting the victorious ruling couple to the subjects and of paying homage to the Egyptian deities. On their return, the two lovers had to separate, but they met again in Rome a year later. In the meantime, Cleopatra had given Caesar a son. To celebrate the divine birth of Ptolemy XV, called Caesarion by the people of Alexandria, Cleopatra held a ceremony in the temple of Armant, close to Thebes. As was the Egyptian tradition, dating back to the 18th Dynasty, Amun-Re was present at the birth of "his son," who was subsequently breastfed by female deities.

Cleopatra went to Rome, where she went with her son and young husband, and stayed for two years, until the plot which brought Caesar's assassination (44 BC). The queen then returned to Egypt and resumed ruling the country alone, but Caesar's death, far from re-establishing the balance of power between Pompey and Mark Antony, created further conflict, although this terminated with an agreement and the foundation of a second triumvirate. Mark Antony undertook a series of victorious campaigns against the Republicans and their Eastern allies, until he found himself almost before Cleopatra, from whom he officially wanted an explanation for her support of Caesar's former allies. Cleopatra, who was anxiously awaiting this moment, made great efforts to ensure that the meeting succeeded once again in swaying the balance in her favor: she obtained the support of Antony against her own relations, and put Ptolemy and Arsinoe to death. Antony stayed in Egypt for a year, during which he and Cleopatra conceived twins, who were born six months after his departure. The foreign situation once again demanded his intervention in Asia against the Parthians, while at home a re-formulation of the agreement with Octavian and Lepidus was ratified by Antony's new marriage to the daughter of Octavian.

In 37 BC, however, Antony returned to Asia and met Cleopatra once again, whom he probably married with Egyptian rites. From this moment, the queen started a new phase in her reign: the couple was practically identified with Isis and Osiris, and

Aphrodite and Dionysius, but the situation in Asia came to a head and Cleopatra left Antony to return to Egypt, where she gave birth to another son, Ptolemy Philadelphus. When Antony's luck ran out, it was the Egyptian army that came to the rescue of the Roman army when they were in difficulty. Cleopatra, at this point, engaged in intense diplomatic activity with nearby countries, in support of Antony's military activities. After a short time the two sovereigns celebrated their victories with a huge event in Alexandria and divided the possessions between Cleopatra, defined "Queen of Queens" and her four children. Naturally this situation could not go unnoticed in Rome, and Octavian accused Antony of giving immense power to a foreigner – and queen of an enemy people.

Even though Antony tried to avoid the conflict, it had become inevitable at this stage, above all after the Roman Senate found out about his will, in which he declared his intention to be buried in Egypt beside Cleopatra. Antony was dismissed from all public appointments, while Octavian declared war on Cleopatra in October 32 BC. Even though the army assembled by Antony

and Cleopatra was larger, the famous battle of Actium in September of 31 BC constituted a first fundamental step toward their defeat. By now they were both considered foreigners and enemies of Rome. Antony succeeded in taking Pelusium and getting close to the gates of Alexandria in the spring of 30 BC. A mad whirl of events followed: rumor had it that Cleopatra – shut in the mausoleum that she had had built for herself – was dead. On hearing this news, denied immediately after, but too late, Antony wounded himself fatally and as he was dying was taken to the mausoleum. Cleopatra wept for Antony and tried in various ways to take her own life but she was watched over by Octavian's men who wanted to take her back to Rome, alive and in chains, as a symbol of great Roman triumph over the enemy from the East. A few days before the departure, however, Cleopatra managed to evade surveillance and killed herself, probably with snake poison brought into the prison in a basket. Notwithstanding this humiliation, Octavian decided to maintain a promise made to Cleopatra and, according to some sources, had her buried with her beloved.

253 The issue (in 32 BC) of this silver denarius celebrated Mark Antony's victories in Armenia, and the ensuing donation of territories to Cleopatra's offspring. The coin, recently named the "Queen of Kings," features an obverse portrait of Cleopatra and on the reverse shows Antony (British Museum, London).

254-255 The Late Period pink granite stele was reutilized by Cleopatra VII who performs offertory rites to Amun and Montu, together with Ptolemy XV, son of the queen and Caesar. In the lower part, the original inscription has been replaced by a Greek and Demotic text (Egyptian Museum, Turin).

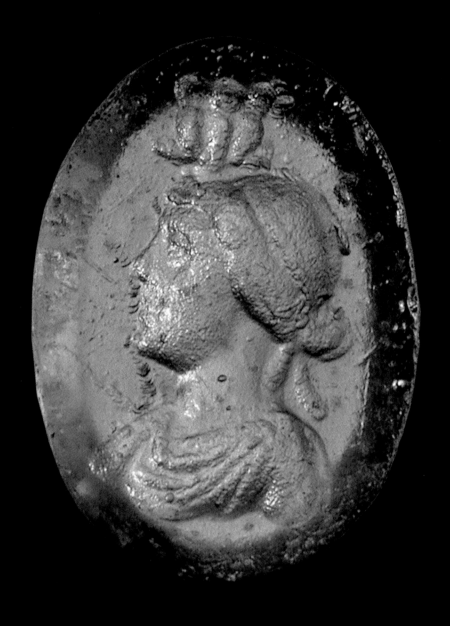

256 This black basalt sculpture, originally considered a portrait of Arsinoe II, has been identified as an image of Cleopatra VII because of the triple uraeus. The queen is holding a double cornucopia in her left hand and the *ankh* insignia, the symbol of life, in her right hand (Hermitage Museum, St. Petersburg).

257 A portrait, carved in blue paste, of a Ptolemaic queen who may very well be Cleopatra VII: both her hairdo with a chignon and, above all, the diadem with the triple uraeus are typical features of images of this famous queen (British Museum, London).

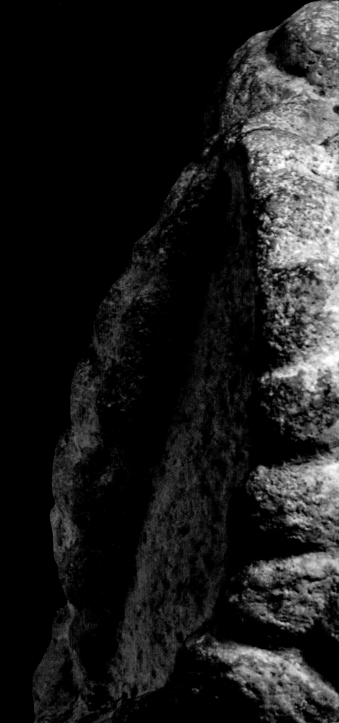

260 BOTTOM SOME OF THE RUINS
FOUND BY THE GROUP OF UNDERWATER
ARCHAEOLOGISTS DURING THEIR
EXPLORATION OF THE WATERS
BETWEEN ALEXANDRIA AND THE
ABU QĪR PENINSULA.

260-261 AND 261 BOTTOM THE
DISCOVERY OF ONE OF THE MANY
SCULPTURES, IN THIS CASE OF A SPHINX,
THAT THE GROUP OF INTERNATIONAL
UNDERWATER ARCHAEOLOGISTS HEADED
BY FRANCK GODDIO BROUGHT TO
LIGHT DURING THEIR EXPLORATIONS
ALONG THE COAST FROM ALEXANDRIA
TO THE ABU QĪR PENINSULA.

262 THIS PORTRAIT OF CLEOPATRA VII
IN PARIAN MARBLE WAS PROBABLY
SCULPTED AS A PART OF A COMPOSITE
LIFE-SIZE STATUE (ANTIKENSAMMLUNG,
BERLIN).

Neither the burial place nor the bodies of the two lovers have ever been found. The area in which the royal quarters were located and where Antony built his place of retreat after the battle of Actium are, however, in a place currently submerged by the Bay of Alexandria, and until a few years ago this locality had never been explored. From 1992 systematic underwater searches of a vast submerged area that goes from Alexandria to the Abu Qïr peninsula (the latter corresponds to the ancient region of Canopus) have been organized, which have shown the presence, in the eastern part of the bay, of architectural structures, stelae, and statues of sovereigns and deities, some of which probably date back to the reign of Ptolemy XII, Cleopatra's father. As far as the eastern sector of the bay of Alexandria is concerned, the quality of the artifacts and the grandeur of the architectural remains induced explorers (the international group of divers directed by Franck Goddio) to declare in 1996 that they were finally before the remains of the location of the palaces and temples of the Ptolomaic sovereigns. Equally extraordinary are the remains of the ancient port of Herakleion, and the colossal works and products brought to light in the entire Canopus area. The study and complete publication of this archaeological documentation will contribute significantly to reconstructing the closure of this extremely long cycle covering the duration of Divine Egyptian Royalty as conceived by priests and theologians three thousand years before.

CHRONOLOGY

This chronological table illustrates the succession of domestic and foreign dynasties and their sovereigns that ruled Egypt. The names of queens and princesses mentioned in the text are presented in SMALL CAPS within their respective dynasties.

PREDYNASTIC PERIOD
(4000–3000 BC)

Naqada I	(4000–3500)
Naqada II	(3500–3100)

Dynasty Zero (c. 3000)
Narmer – NEITHHOTEP

EARLY DYNASTIC PERIOD
(2920–2575 BC)

1st Dynasty (2920–2770)
Aha (Menes ?)
Djer – HERINEITH
Djet – MERINEITH
Den
Adjib
Semerkhet
Qaa

2nd Dynasty (2770–2649)
Hetepsekhemui
Raneb – SHEPSESTIPET
Nynetjer
Peribsen
Khasekhem (Khasekhemui) – NIMAATHAPI

OLD KINGDOM
(2649–2152 BC)

3rd Dynasty (2649–2575)

Sanakht	2649–2630
Djoser (Netjerkhet)	2630–2611
Sekhemkhet	2611–2603
Khaba	2603–2600
Huni	2600–2575

4th Dynasty (2575–2465)

Snefru – HETEPHERES I	2575–2551
Khufu	2551–2528
Djedefre – HETEPHERES II	2528–2520
Khafre – MERSEANKH III	2520–2494
Menkaure – KHAMERERNEBTY II	2494–2472
Shepseskaf – KHENTKAUS I	2472–2465

5th Dynasty (2465–2323)

Userkaf	2465–2458
Sahure	2458–2446
Neferirkare Kakai	2446–2426
Shepseskare	2426–2419
Neferefre	2419–2416
Niuserre	2416–2392
Menkauhor	2392–2388
Djedkare Isesi	2388–2356
Unis	2356–2323

6th Dynasty (2323–2152)

Teti	2323–2291
Pepi I – ANKHNESMERIRE I	2289–2255
Merenre – ANKHNESMERIRE II	2255–2246
Pepi II – NEITH	2246–2152
NITOCRIS	

FIRST INTERMEDIATE PERIOD
(2152–2065 BC)

7th Dynasty

8th Dynasty (2152–2135)

9th and 10th Dynasties (2135–2040)

11th Dynasty – first part (2135–2065)

Mentuhotep I	
Antef I	
Antef II	2123–2073
Antef III	2073–2065

MIDDLE KINGDOM
(2065–1781 BC)

11th Dynasty – second part (2065–1994)

Mentuhotep II – TEM, NEFERU, ASHAYT, KAUIT	
Nebhepetre	2065–2014
Mentuhotep III	2014–2001
Mentuhotep IV	2001–1994

12th Dynasty (1994–1781)

Amenemhat I	1994–1964
Senusret I	1964–1929
Amenemhat II – KHNUMIT, ITA	1929–1898
Senusret II – KHENEMETNEFERHEDJET, NOFRET, SATHATHORIUNET	1898–1881
Senusret III – WERET, MERERET	1881–1842
Amenemhat III – NEFRUPTAH	1842–1794
Amenemhat IV	1793–1785
SOBEKNEFERU	1785–1781

SECOND INTERMEDIATE PERIOD
(1781–1550 BC)

13th Dynasty (1781–1650)

14th Dynasty (1710–1650)

15th Dynasty (1650–1550)
Main Hyksos kings:
Salitis
Sheshi
Jaqobher
Khayan
Apopi
Khamudi

16th Dynasty (1650–1550)

17th Dynasty (1650–1550)
15 Theban monarchs, of whom the most important are:
Antef V
Sobekemsaef I
Sobekemsaef II
Antef VI
Antef VII
Seqenenra Tao I – TETISHERI
Seqenenra Tao II – AHHOTEP I
Kamose

NEW KINGDOM
(1550–1075 BC)

18th Dynasty (1550–1291)

Ahmose – AHMES-NEFERTARI	1550–1525
Amenhotep I – AHMES-MERITAMUN	1525–1504
Thutmosis I	1504–1492
Thutmosis II – ASET	1492–1479
HATSHEPSUT – NEFERURE	1479–1458
Thutmosis III – MANUWAI, MANHATA, MARUTA	1479–1425
Amenhotep II – TIA	1424–1397
Thutmosis IV	1397–1387
Amenhotep III – TIYE, SITAMUN	1387–1350
Amenhotep IV/ Akhenaten – NEFERTITI, MERITATEN	1350–1333
Smenkhare	1335–1333
Tutankhamun – ANKHESENAMUN	1333–1323
Ay	1323–1319
Horemheb	1319–1291

19th Dynasty (1291–1185)

Ramesses I	1291–1289
Seti I	1289–1279
Ramesses II – NEFERTARI, ISTNOFRET, BINTANAT, MERITAMUN, NEBETTAUI, HENUTMIRE, MAATHORNEFERURE	1279–1212
Merenptah	1212–1202
Amenemes	1202–1199
Seti II	1199–1193
Siptah	1193–1187
Tausret	1193–1185

20th Dynasty (1185–1075)

Sethnakht	1185–1184
Ramesses III	1184–1153
Ramesses IV	1153–1147
Ramesses V	1147–1143
Ramesses VI	1143–1135
Ramesses VII	1135–1127
Ramesses VIII	1127–1126
Ramesses IX	1126–1108
Ramesses X	1108–1104
Ramesses XI	1104–1075

THIRD INTERMEDIATE PERIOD
(1075–664 BC)

21st Dynasty (1075–945)

Smendes I – MAATKARE	1075–1049
Neferkare	1049–1043
Psusennes I	1045–994
Amenemope	994–985
Osorkon the Elder	985–979
Siamun	979–960
Psusennes II	960–945

22nd Dynasty (945–718)

Sheshonq I	945–924
Osorkon I	924–899
Sheshonq II	c. 890
Takelot I	889–883
Osorkon II	883–850
Takelot II – KAROMAMA	853–827
Sheshonq III	827–775
Pamy	775–767
Sheshonq V	767–729
Osorkon IV	729–718

23rd Dynasty (820–718)

Petubasti	820–795
Sheshonq IV	795–788
Osorkon III	788–760
Takelot III	765–756
Rudamun	752–718

24th Dynasty (730–712)

Tefnakht	730–718
Boccoris	718–712

25th Dynasty (775–653)

Alara	775–765
Kashta – AMENIRDIS I	765–745
Pi(ankhi) – SHEPENUPET II	745–713
Shabaka	713–698
Shabataka	698–690
Taharqa – AMENIRDIS II	690–664
Tanutamani	664–653

LATE PERIOD
(664–332 BC)

26th Dynasty (664–525)

Psammetichus I – NITOCRIS I	664–610
Necho	610–595
Psammetichus II	595–589
Aprie	589–570
Amasi	570–526
Psammetichus III	526–525

27th Dynasty (525–404)

Cambyses	525–522
Darius I	521–486
Xerxes I	486–465
Artaxerses I	465–424
Xerxes II	424
Darius II	423–405
Artaxerses II	405–404

28th Dynasty (404–399)

Amyrtaeus	404–399

29th Dynasty (399–380)

Nepherites I	399–393
Hakor	393–380

30th Dynasty (380–342)

Nectanebo I	380–362
Tachos	362–360
Nectanebo II	360–342

31st Dynasty (342–332)

Artaxerses III	342–338
Arses	338–336
Darius III	336–332

HELLENISTIC PERIOD
(332–30 BC)

The Macedonians (332–305)

Alexander the Great	332–323
Philip Arrhidaeus	323–317
Alexander IV	317–305

Ptolemaic Dynasty (305–30)

Ptolemy I Soter	305–282
Ptolemy II Philadelphus – ARSINOE II	285–246
Ptolemy III Evergetes – BERENICE III	246–222
Ptolemy IV Philopator – ARSINOE III	222–205
Ptolemy V Epiphanes – CLEOPATRA I	205–180
Ptolemy VI Philometor – CLEOPATRA II	180–164, 163–145
Ptolemy VII Neos Philopator	145
Ptolemy VIII Evergetes	170–163, 145–116
Ptolemy IX Soter	116–110, 109–107, 88–80
Ptolemy X Alexander	110–109, 107–88
Ptolemy XI Alexander	80
Ptolemy XII Neos Dionysos	80–58, 55–51
BERENICE IV	58–55
CLEOPATRA VII PHILOPATOR	51–30
Ptolemy XV Caesarion	36–30

265 THE GODDESS SEKHMET, A DECORATION ON A TUTANKHAMUN PECTORAL.

INDEX

PHOTO CREDITS

ACKNOWLEDGMENTS

The author wishes to thank her colleague and friend Alessia Amenta for inviting her to take part in this project; Giorgio Ferrero for his precious help in all the stages of development; and last, but not least, her husband Davide for his constant consideration of the work and his meticulous revision of the first draft.

The publisher wishes to thank His Excellency Farouk Hosny, Egyptian Minister of Culture; Dr. Zahi Hawass, Secretary General of the Supreme Council of Antiquities and Director of the Giza Pyramids Excavation; Mr. Sabry Abdel Aziz Qater, Director General of the Egyptian Antiquities Sector; Dr. Wafaa el-Sadiq, Director of the Museum of Egyptian Antiquities, Cairo.

© 2008 White Star S.p.A.
Via Candido Sassone, 22/24 - 13100 Vercelli, Italy - www.whitestar.it

TRANSLATION: ANGELA ARNONE

ISBN 978-88-544-0334-5

REPRINTS: 1 2 3 4 5 6   12 11 10 09 08

Color separation: Fotomec, Turin - Printed in China

272 QUEEN NEFERTARI, DEPICTED ON A WALL OF HER TOMB.